WLY   16.50

W9-CKJ-446

WLY   16.50

*A Pictorial
Life Story*

Winston Churchill

Authorized by the WINSTON CHURCHILL FOUNDATION

By ELIZABETH LONGFORD

RAND McNALLY & COMPANY

CHICAGO   NEW YORK   SAN FRANCISCO

JACKET PHOTOGRAPHS
Front cover: KARSH, OTTAWA
Back cover: GODFREY ARGENT

LIBRARY OF CONGRESS CATALOGING IN PUBLICATION DATA

Longford, Elizabeth Harman Pakenham, Countess of, 1906-
  WINSTON CHURCHILL.

  1. Churchill, Sir Winston Leonard Spencer, 1874–1965.
DA566.9.C5L66   942.082'092'4[B]   74-13104
ISBN 0-528-81822-8

Copyright © 1974 by RAND MCNALLY & COMPANY

All rights reserved

Printed in the UNITED STATES OF AMERICA
by RAND MCNALLY & COMPANY

First printing, 1974

*For
Frank
and
Jock*

Contents

Foreword

THIS YEAR, 1974, is the centenary of the birth of Winston Spencer Churchill. In this preface to the pictorial record and commentary on his life, I will attempt no biography but will try to set down some impressions of this remarkable man based on our years of work together.

Winston Churchill will always be remembered for his leadership of his country, the British Commonwealth and Empire, and the free world in the critical years of the Second World War. While he had not the power at his command to defeat the Nazi tyranny unaided, he had the vision, the courage, and the genius to make victory possible.

In January, 1938, while I was Foreign Secretary, and on a brief holiday in the south of France, Churchill, who had recently given me strong support on one or two occasions in the House of Commons, invited me to luncheon with Lloyd George as the only other guest. The three of us discussed for a long time the darkening world scene, the threats of the two European dictators, and our relations with the United States.

It was therefore natural that after my resignation only a few weeks later, Churchill and I should foregather, because we each knew that we shared the same anxieties and agreed as to how to meet them. So it proved then, and so it proved almost without a break over the next 20 years. As he once remarked long afterwards, you could put us in separate rooms, put the same question to us on almost any topic of foreign affairs, and, nine times out of ten, our answers would be identical.

Courage for some sudden act, maybe in the heat of battle, we all respect; but there is that still rarer courage which can sustain repeated disappointment, unexpected failure, and shattering defeat. Churchill had that too, and he had need of it, not for a day, but for weeks and months and years.

Looking back now at the war, victory may seem to have been certain. It was not always so. I saw much of Churchill then, often many times a day, not only at official meetings but in such periods of comparative relaxation as there were, at meals and late into the night. There is the dogged type that if set upon the right course can hold to it. Churchill was much more than that. He felt deeply

9

every blow of fortune and every gleam of hope. Alert, eager, and questing as his temper was, he could hold on through all tides and tempests. He sensed danger for his country with the touch of the artist and the knowledge of the historian.

Churchill as Prime Minister was daunting and indefatigable, but he had very little use for a mere "yes-man." He might be glad for the moment that someone had made no difficulties. His later reflections, however, were not likely to be complimentary to the individual concerned, particularly if he thought him guilty of trying to anticipate what the Prime Minister wanted him to say. Scores of times Churchill remarked after we had been working over some draft, perhaps of a speech or of a telegram or despatch, "Two heads are better than one." He always liked to work that way. Clear and firm as his opinions usually were, it is wrong to suppose that they were never subject to modification by others. Sometimes attempts to persuade him to change his view might lead to sharp differences and even to stormy exchanges; then after a while the effect of the argument, if it had been well marshalled, would have its influence on his judgment. At the next meeting, it might be that the colleague who had disagreed with him would find that Churchill had not only taken account of his views, but had perhaps made some part of them, or all of them, his own. Though this could be disconcerting, it was all part of his endearing humour and humanity.

Another characteristic which was invaluable in the conduct of the war was his refusal to accept a technical argument until he had probed its validity. He would insist on testing it to determine whether it was well-founded or shallow, and it was at these times that he could be at his best. There were certainly occasions before the war when we should have benefited from this quality at our Cabinet meetings.

As the world knows, Churchill loved to read history and to write it, but that is not all. He was literally soaked in history, and it was fascinating when some new problem came along to see how his mind in approaching it would delve into the resources of his capacious memory for some example or some experience of the past which would help to guide us.

The discussion of history with Churchill was, therefore, always illuminating. I remember one evening in the dark days of 1940 when I was dining alone with him. We were sitting after dinner debating which period of history we would have preferred to live in had the choice been ours. He favoured the age of Queen Anne and of Marlborough's wars, I preferred that of Pitt and the struggle with Napoleon; we were both attracted by the first Elizabethan age. After we had been talking in this fashion for a while, Churchill concluded: "Of course, of all of them this is the greatest, this is the one in which to live." And he meant it, at a time when our fortunes, though bravely upheld, were at their nadir.

It was this sense of history, as well as ancestry, that influenced Churchill in his absorbed interest in the United States, whether the campaigns of the Civil War or some intricate issue of domestic politics was the immediate topic of the hour.

Churchill was always eager for an opportunity to visit the United States, not only because he liked to strengthen the alliance by these occasional journeys, but because he found refreshment in contacts there. He felt instinctively and had learned from experience that, when truly together, our two countries could achieve so much more than the sum of our individual efforts. He knew the United States, and what we may call the American mind, more intimately than any other Englishman. When talking at home among his own countrymen, he would often illustrate his themes from his American contacts and travels. Probably he owed his formidable constitution to his transatlantic forebears; certainly he was a living example of how to get the best of both worlds.

Statesman, warrior, writer, and painter, his genius had few parallels ever. These gifts, expressed with such tenacity and courage, made his leadership unique in quality and strength.

Avon

"That Boy"

I can never do anything right. . . . I suppose I shall go on being treated as "that boy" till I am 50 years old.
WINSTON, AGED 18, TO HIS MOTHER

POPPERFOTO

Winston Churchill was born in a palace. It was Blenheim Palace, the superb gift of the nation to his illustrious ancestor John Churchill, first Duke of Marlborough. Winston was a natural romantic rather than a grandee. "Would you like a Dukedom or anything like that?" Queen Elizabeth II engagingly asked him when he retired from the premiership in 1955. Mr. Churchill would not like to be a duke. Nevertheless, he was romantic about dukes, as he was about so many other things. Among them, his Kentish home, Chartwell, where he spent 40 happy years—"A day from Chartwell is a day wasted;" the horse—"No hour of life is lost that is spent in the saddle;" the ordinary British sentence—"a noble thing;" the Anglo-Saxon character, which he first discovered during the Battle of Omdurman—"My faith in our race & blood was much strengthened;" and above all, the English-speaking peoples.

His enthusiasms welled up from within him like springs on a great watershed. Out gushed the sparkling streams, giving a romantic glitter to all they touched. Without these gifts of vision and enthusiasm, his genius might have foundered in a tough childhood.

Winston Leonard Spencer-Churchill* was born two months prematurely at 1:30 a.m. on Monday, November 30, 1874, in a bedroom at Blenheim which may still be seen. His 20-year-old mother, Jennie, was staying with her ducal in-laws and was supposed to have precipitated the birth by over-activity during the weekend. This is not obviously so, since Winston's brother, John (Jack) Strange Spencer-Churchill, was also born prematurely.

Jennie had intended to produce her first-born in London. Fate, however, took a hand. To be born in a palace or a log cabin —or a manger—is fine. But to be born at No. 48 Charles Street, Mayfair, his parents' first London home, would not have given Churchill that romantic send-off which was clearly his due.

Facing page: Interior of an armoured train used during the Boer War in South Africa. In 1899, Churchill's trip in such a train led to his capture by the Boers; his thrilling escape made him a popular hero in Britain.

---

* In later years, the family tended to drop the hyphen from the surname.

POPPERFOTO

Lord Randolph Churchill, father of Winston S. Churchill and younger son of the 7th Duke of Marlborough.

The father of this baby-in-a-hurry was Lord Randolph Churchill, second surviving son of the 7th Duke of Marlborough. He had fallen in love at first sight with "the dark one" of two lovely Jerome sisters, Jennie and Clara, whom he met at Cowes. Their father, Leonard Jerome, was a prominent figure in American turf and yachting circles who had made three fortunes and lost two-and-a-half. At 80, Winston was to read Anita Leslie's *The Fabulous Leonard Jerome* and to revel in what he found there. "A really remarkable man," he said of his grandfather; "he did exactly what he liked—and he liked what he did." Winston proudly described his Jerome ancestors as all "very fierce," adding, "I'm the only tame one they've produced."

Leonard Jerome had at first welcomed his daughter's engagement, calling Lord Randolph "young, ambitious, uncorrupted"—all good American qualities. But when the Marlboroughs objected to their son's choosing an American bride, Jerome was properly incensed. "We have nothing to equal this," King George III had once said when he saw the Marlboroughs' palace. Now Leonard Jerome rightly felt that the English aristocracy had nothing to equal his Jennie. Fortunately, love vanquished all. Randolph and Jennie were married on April 15, 1874, at the British Embassy in Paris, Jennie carrying a parasol of white lace to match her dress.

POPPERFOTO

The bedroom at Blenheim Palace where Winston was born on November 30, 1874.

Randolph described his baby son as "wonderfully pretty" with dark hair and eyes. He had probably never seen a newborn baby before and wrongly thought the child had inherited Jennie's lustrous dark hair and deep grey eyes. Actually, Winston was to have pale auburn curls and eyes of light blue. In later years, his daughter Sarah was to call them "those strange pallid eyes."

Winston's neglect by his youthful, self-absorbed parents is today a well-established fact. His biographer-son, Randolph Spencer Churchill, used the adjective "neglectful" of their behaviour and "bleak" of Winston's youth. Anita Leslie, granddaughter of the third beautiful Jerome sister, Leonie Leslie, and young Randolph's cousin, said of Jennie: "She was only twenty and her interests did not center in the nursery." There were no baby clothes ready for this premature child—an excusable failure—but the clothes provided throughout his babyhood were denounced by his nanny, Mrs. Everest, as chronically outgrown and "shabby." His mother was not interested.

The interests of both parents, indeed, were focused entirely upon that gay and sometimes raffish world created by the Prince of Wales, afterwards King Edward VII. However, in 1876 Lord Randolph fell foul of the Prince over a society divorce scandal, and London turned suddenly inhospitable. In order to remove the family from this hostile atmosphere, the Duke of Marlborough accepted the post of Viceroy in Ireland, taking Randolph along as his secretary.

Winston's earliest memory of his dazzling mother came from those childhood days in Dublin: "My picture of her in Ireland is in a riding habit, fitting like a skin and often beautifully spotted with mud. She and my father hunted continually on their large horses . . . ."

Shortly after Jack's birth in February, 1880, the family returned to England, though four more years would pass before the breach with the Prince of Wales was healed. Winston could later look back on his father's years of social ostracism as a partial blessing. These years had given Lord Randolph an independent spirit. Misfortune may have embittered his genial nature and turned him against "rank and authority;" but it had spurred him on to develop "popular sympathies" and to espouse "democratic causes."

Back in London, Lord Randolph plunged into party politics with a brilliance, impetuousness, and gift for oratorical invective that were soon to make him a national figure. There were at this

THE BETTMANN ARCHIVE

Jennie Jerome, the lovely American who became Lady Randolph Churchill. Dark and lithe, she was likened by one admirer to a panther.

17

time three major parties in the British Parliament: the Conservatives (Tories), the party of the Right; the Liberals, the party of the Left; and the Irish Nationalists. Lord Randolph was soon organising his splinter group, the "Fourth Party," and inventing "Tory Democracy."

Winston, meanwhile, had no such fun. On November 3, 1882, he was sent to St. George's School, Ascot. "Winston's schooldays," wrote his son, "were the only unhappy part of his life. His pugnacious and rebellious nature never adapted itself to discipline." The horrors of St. George's included discipline which bordered on sadism. It was practised by a headmaster who died young of heart failure, no doubt worn out by his vigorous exertions with the cane. Winston's sensitive white skin (in which he was later to take pride) was reddened by weals. When flogged for stealing sugar, he retaliated by kicking the headmaster's "sacred" straw hat to bits.

At the end of the first term, he ranked 11th in a class of 11. His report called him greedy, and his conduct was described as exceedingly bad throughout his attendance at this snobbish version of Dickens's infamous "Dotheboys Hall." The tragedy was that it took his parents so long to discover the truth. When they did, he was sent to a friendly school run by two ladies at Brighton. Here, notwithstanding the care and climate, he caught pneumonia at 11 and nearly died. Next came Harrow. It had never seemed likely that this great public school would number among its pupils another name as famous as Lord Byron's—until Churchill arrived.

Again a bad first-term report; he was remarkable for "phenomenal slovenliness" and "negligence." There was a gleam of hope, however. He was very good at history. And he was already susceptible to patriotic minstrelsy. The Harrow School Songs made him wonder "with intensity" how he could do something glorious for his country:

> *God give us bases to guard or beleaguer,*
> *Games to play out whether earnest or fun;*
> *Fights for the fearless and goals for the eager,*
> *Twenty and thirty and forty years on.*

Fifty years on, he was telling his son Randolph about this early inspiration, as together they drove home from a wartime Harrow sing-song.

Macaulay's *Lays of Ancient Rome*, of which he learned 1,200 lines for a prize, struck the same chords in his schoolboy heart:

18

Then none was for a party;
    Then all were for the state;
Then the great man helped the poor,
    And the poor man loved the great;
Then lands were fairly portioned;
    Then spoils were fairly sold:
The Romans were like brothers
    In the brave days of old.

Here in resounding verse was the pith of Churchill's political philosophy. His goal would be to transplant that imagined golden age of brotherhood into the real Europe and America of the 1940s.

At 13, Winston was showing signs of a distinctive interest in words. One letter to his mother written after Christmas, 1888, spoke of a model theatre, a gift from his two American aunts, as being "a source of unparalleled amusement." His exchequer invariably needed "replenishing;" good news was "pleasing intelligence;" his knowledge of packing was "limited"—so might his old nanny, Mrs. Everest, please come down to Harrow to help him pack at the end of term? And bring ten shillings journey money and his best trousers for Speech Day, when he goes up for his Macaulay recitation prize?

Winston's questions must surely provoke in return a key question affecting his schooldays. Did his "Dearest Mamma," or for that matter Papa, go down to Harrow on that July day of 1888 to watch their smartly trousered son accept his award—a portentous prize to be carried off by a small boy in the bottom form? Did they encourage him, show the interest of normal Victorian parents? The answer is consistently no.

At this point, it is necessary to enter one caveat in regard to this couple's apparently bland selfishness. The impression is sometimes given that they were entirely absorbed in one another, in politics, or in pleasure. That may have been so while Winston was a small boy. But by the summer of 1886 a tragic change had come about in his father's health and therefore in his parents' mutual love. (This we know from Anita Leslie's biography of Jennie.) Lord Randolph had to tell his partially estranged wife of the true reason for his coldness—the disease which was to cause general paralysis in seven years' time and to kill him in 1895. Burdened as she was with this terrible secret, Lady Randolph deserves nothing but sympathy. Any picture of her as a happy, heartless social butterfly must be scrapped.

IMPERIAL WAR MUSEUM

POPPERFOTO

*Winston at seven,
with the characteristic
look of debonair
defiance.*

*A painting of Winston,
aged five, in Ireland.*

*As a fifteen-year-old
Harrovian, Winston
entered the Army Class.
"This orientation was
entirely due to my
collection of
soldiers."*

RADIO TIMES HULTON PICTURE LIBRARY

SYNDICATION INTERNATIONAL

Commissioned in the 4th Hussars, 1895. Churchill always felt nostalgic about cavalry. "It is a shame that war should have flung all this aside in its greedy, base, opportunist march, and should turn instead to chemists in spectacles."

POPPERFOTO/CONWAY PICTURE LIBRARY

Winston is on the left, about to leave Sandhurst in 1894. "Since Sandhurst," he wrote, "I have never had time to turn round."

Winston Churchill's son, Randolph, has rightly asserted that his father was not "stupid" as a schoolboy but "mutinous." He reacted against authority at school and therefore did not work. This was not how Lord Randolph saw the situation. Convinced that his elder son was too stupid to read for the Bar, he finally decided to have him made into a soldier. At least Winston was enjoying the Rifle Corps at Harrow. And Lord Randolph had earlier noticed that Winston showed intense concentration when playing with toy soldiers on the nursery floor.

Concentration was indeed among Winston's greatest gifts. Nevertheless, his father, in choosing a military career for this supposed dunce, did not rise above the rest of his parental performance. One is reminded of Wellington's mother contemplating that other awkward genius with the words, "food for powder and nothing more." From September, 1889, therefore, Winston followed Harrow's "Army Class" curriculum, which was to prepare him for passing into the Royal Military College at Sandhurst.

One question remains to be answered before Churchill can be followed with understanding to Sandhurst and thence into the Army. How did parental neglect, added to his unhappy schooldays, affect his development?

He did not blame his mother. Despite all evidence to the contrary, he persuaded himself that she loved him as extravagantly as he adored her. "Now you know, I was always your darling . . . ." Years later, he was to remember their relationship in a more truthful but still glamorous light: "My mother always seemed to me a fairy princess: a radiant being possessed of limitless riches and power. She shone for me like the Evening Star. I loved her dearly —but at a distance."

Lord Randolph also kept his son at a distance. Winston recalled in his fragment of autobiography, *My Early Life*, how he had once offered to give his father secretarial help—and been frozen to stone by Lord Randolph's cold response. Towards the end, it is true, the stricken statesman unbent a little. As he drove with his wife and son to the station at the start of his last macabre journey, he patted Winston on the knee. Anita Leslie described this as "almost the only affectionate gesture that Lord Randolph had ever shown his son."

Notwithstanding this coldness, young Winston had felt the excitement generated by the meteoric career which carried his father from the depths of "exile" in 1880 to the heights as Chancellor of the Exchequer in 1886. He had also shared the disillusionment which followed, when Lord Randolph's threat to resign from the Cabinet was unexpectedly accepted. After Lord Randolph's death, Winston was to found his own early political career on a kind of filial Holy Grail: the quest for his father's posthumous political fulfillment. Thus Winston's own warm emotionalism transformed his state of "rejection" by his father into a crusade on behalf of the rejector. It proved a most positive method of compensation.

Winston was saved from psychological damage by his relationship with his nanny, Mrs. Everest. While Lord Randolph kept him at a distance and from a distance he adored Lady Randolph, Mrs. Everest loomed warm and close. Above—his mother, the "Evening Star," shining remote and hard as the diamonds in her hair; below —the huge earthbound security of Everest. She was, of course, a mother substitute. Her nickname of "Woomany," however, was a childish version of "woman," not a Freudian slip. Instances abound of Winston's reliance on Woomany's devotion. One must suffice. When at 16 he took the Preliminary Examination for the Royal Military College at Sandhurst, he had a choice of three English essay subjects: Rowing versus Riding, Advertisements, or The American Civil War. He wrote to his mother, "I did the last." This choice in itself is not without interest, in view of his future absorption in Anglo-American relations. Equally significant, however, is the next sentence: "Show this to Everest as she is awfully keen."

When the Duchess of Marlborough finally proposed to "pack off" Mrs. Everest without a pension, he wrote with unusual sharpness to his mother: "I think such proceedings cruel & rather mean." Winston made her an allowance. He sat with her as she died in 1895—the same year as his Jerome grandmother and his father. He might have been writing Mrs. Everest's epitaph when, in his novel *Savrola*, he spoke of the love of women like her for their foster-children as perhaps "the only disinterested affection in the world." It was an argument, he wrote, against materialism and a proof of "man's high destiny."

In time to come, he would legislate with his nanny in mind. His work for Old Age Pensioners was not so much to rescue a host of faceless people as to commemorate the devoted service of one specific old lady, Mrs. Everest. This was how Churchill's mind worked.

It was Mrs. Everest who had given Winston the best reasons for getting into Sandhurst. "I hope you will try & work well dearest this term to please his Lordship . . . & your Mamma . . . & disappoint some of your relations who prophesy a future of profligacy for you. . . ."

When, on his third try at the Preliminary Examination, he did manage to scrape in, his father felt it his duty to modify his son's exultation. His "discreditable" results were part and parcel of Winston's hitherto "idle useless unprofitable life" and his drift towards becoming "a mere social wastrel," destined to lead "a shabby unhappy & futile existence." And all of it, from first to last, stemmed from Winston's "slovenly happy-go-lucky harum scarum style of work."

Winston replied to this tirade with surprising restraint. "My extremely low place in passing *in* will have *no* effect whatever on my chance there. . . ." Then came the inevitable harum scarum touch at the end: "P.S. Excuse smudge &c. . . ."

Churchill had left Harrow with one school prize, the Macaulay recitation, and one athletic crown, the Public Schools' Fencing Championship. This latter was a tribute to his dash rather than muscle or dexterity. For the rest, he was never promoted from the Lower School. Nevertheless, his own later accounts of his youthful humiliations were exaggerated. A confirmed romantic, he much preferred to imagine a situation where brilliant success was born of unmitigated failure.

His character had changed little while at Harrow. Indeed, the confident, if not already truculent, front he showed to the world was as evident at seven as at seventeen. Lady Constance Leslie, his Aunt Leonie's mother-in-law, described him to H. Rider Haggard as "uppish." All the same, Winston was "really a very interesting being," and so Lady Constance risked introducing Winston to his favourite author. His most notorious instance of "push" at Harrow was when Winston the new boy pushed Leo Amery the exalted but deceptively small sixth-former into the swimming pool. Still uppish and interesting as ever, young Winston Churchill entered Sandhurst in September, 1893.

Two things happened at Sandhurst which deeply affected Churchill's future. He learned for the first time to accept discipline: the "very strict" external discipline of a military college and the voluntary discipline of hard work. As a result, he passed out 20th in a class of 130, quite a change from his place of entry—92nd out of 102.

Secondly, he steeped himself in the romance of war. How frustrating to think that "the age of wars between civilised nations had come to an end for ever." His only hope was that Afghans, Dervishes, or Zulus might some day "put up a show."

Hardly was he equipped to receive a commission in December, 1894, when his father died on January 24, 1895. Actually, Lord Randolph's death came as a happy release for his elder son as well as for himself. His illness had made him impossibly irritable, so that Winston had long been writing such things as, "I can never do anything right . . . . I suppose I shall go on being treated as 'that boy' till I am 50 years old." At his father's death he was 20. Less than a month later, with his mother's efficient help, he had obtained a commission in a cavalry regiment, the 4th (Queen's Own) Hussars.

Jennie, Winston, and Jack were alone in the world. They had very little money. Jennie was still buying herself £200 ball dresses and Winston receiving a £200 horse from his Marlborough grandmother, but neither could really afford the kind of life which went with these princely purchases. Winston's pay was £120 a year.

Churchill with his polo ponies in India.

POPPERFOTO

Characteristically, he did not spend his first long leave in fox-hunting—the hussars' usual pastime—but in seeing the world. By November, 1895, he was in New York, sitting at the feet of Bourke Cockran, a remarkable political orator related to Jennie by marriage. From Cockran's conversation Churchill learned the romance of verbal "rotundity" and "antithesis;" from Cockran's country he learned to admire realism. "This is a very great country my dear Jack," he wrote to his brother. "Not pretty or romantic but great and utilitarian. There seems to be no such thing as reverence or tradition. Everything is eminently practical . . . ." But as his raptures swelled, Churchill was clearly transmuting American utilitarianism into the greatest romance of all.

At the end of a lyrical week, Churchill embarked for Cuba. Through typical "push" he had fitted himself up with a contract to describe his adventures in the London *Daily Graphic* at £5 a column. Another little push and he obtained permission to visit the front, where the then Spanish masters of Cuba were endeavouring to put down an insurrection. He celebrated his 21st birthday by hearing shots fired in anger for the first time. Having earned £25, which he spent on an eighteenth century book of fables, he returned to England.

"I am for makeshifts and expediency," he had once written to Bourke Cockran. He considered his Cuban adventure an expedient. The only marked effect it had on his future was to teach him to take a siesta and to launch the totally erroneous legend that he had fought for Spain against America in the Spanish-American War. But at least Cuba had been real life—a glimpse into the "Aladdin's Cave" which the world had seemed to him on leaving Sandhurst.

In September, 1896, he joined his regiment in India. He did not willingly choose this "useless and unprofitable exile." Yet he had to keep himself, and so India, too, was an expedient. He longed to follow his father's profession and "beat my sword into an iron despatch box." But sword it had to remain—until, on scrambling ashore at Bombay, he dislocated his right shoulder. After that, he could no longer rely on his sword in a crisis. The accident turned out to be one of his lucky breaks. For at the Battle of Omdurman, the lethal pistol which he flourished instead of a sword probably saved his life.

The India of 1896–97 was then undoubtedly the brightest jewel in the British imperial crown, a great sub-continent whose myriad inhabitants were ruled by a few thousand British officials and

POPPERFOTO

dominated by a small British-officered army. But India proved to be as frustrating as Churchill had feared. Polo was glorious fun—and he was good at it, even though he played with his right upper arm strapped to his side in deference to his dislocated shoulder. But polo was not politics. He began a course of serious reading and studied the political scene at long range. "I am a Liberal in all but name," he wrote to his mother. He shared the Liberals' belief in the vote, universal education, the eight-hour day, and graduated income tax. But his Liberalism was only relative to his surroundings. When he came home on leave and was invited to deliver his maiden speech on behalf of the Conservative Primrose League at a manor near Bath, he was delighted to do so. The Liberals he called "discredited faddists."

India was at last "putting on a show." A frontier war had broken out at Malakand in Afghanistan. Churchill, now 22, got round that heroically named warrior, Sir Bindon Blood, to let him serve there. At the same time he became war correspondent on the *Daily Telegraph*. "I have faith in my star," he wrote, "—that is that I am intended to do something in the world."

This is Churchill's first recorded mention of his "star." Like Napoleon, Wellington, Cecil Rhodes, or General Gordon, Churchill held himself to be a man of destiny. This belief was to grow. In 1897, his aspirations were still comparatively modest. He did not expect, he said, to win the Victoria Cross, but he did need a

The India which Churchill found as a young officer. Representatives of the British Raj at a hunt breakfast, 1899.

27

medal. Only publicity would enable him to make big money with his pen and so escape from the sword. And after all, he had personally felled four of the enemy while trying to rescue a wounded sepoy in the Mamund Valley. Foolishly daring, he admitted, but "I play for high stakes . . . ."

For that bit of daring, he was mentioned by Sir Bindon Blood in despatches. He was also "mentioned" unfavourably at home as a "pusher" and "medal-hunter." What did he care? This was only the beginning of the great push which was to be his life. Now, at 23, with the declaration to his mother "I believe in myself," he turned to the pen. His first book, *The Story of the Malakand Field Force,* was published in 1898.

Yet the medals he craved were not entirely a means to other ends. "I am more ambitious," he said, "for a reputation for personal courage than anything else in the world." That thought, added his biographer Randolph, was to be the basis of all his political achievement.

"It is a pushing age and we must shove with the best." With these encouraging words to his mother, he opened the year 1898. Somehow she must get him transferred to Egypt. In India "the outlook is I fear pacific." In Egypt things were different. Although technically not part of the British Empire, Egypt was no more than an imperial satellite. In the eighties, Dervishes of the Anglo-Egyptian Sudan had found a national leader in the Mahdi, had captured Khartoum, killed the British General Gordon, and threatened southern Egypt. Now there was to be a glorious punitive expedition led by the renowned Kitchener. It would be a river war —up the Nile. Thanks to his mother and Sir Evelyn Wood of the War Office, Churchill was posting up the Nile by August. But it was really his own relentless "daemon" which had got him there. And not only there and attached to the 21st Lancers, but paid £15 a column by the *Morning Post* into the bargain.

Kitchener efficiently routed the primitive Dervish army at the Battle of Omdurman. Churchill's dramatic part in the action fully justified his hopes. Before the battle, he had admitted, "I may be killed," adding, "I do not think so." Twenty-one Lancers were killed and 49 seriously wounded during the famous charge, but Churchill's star (and Mauser pistol) led him through unscathed. His thrilling account of his adventure with the 21st Lancers gave his next book, *The River War,* an immediate and lasting appeal. He wrote (but not for the book, for this was still the Victorian age): "Opposite me they were about 4 deep. But they all fell knocked A.O.T. [arse over tip] and we passed through without any sort of shock."

Before the battle, he had been thrown a bottle of champagne from a Nile gunboat by Lieutenant David Beatty. Many years later, Churchill was to ask Beatty, now an admiral, what the charge had looked like from the gunboat. The Admiral replied with the clear-eyed good humour which the sister service deserved: "It looked like plum duff: brown currants [the Lancers' brown uniforms] scattered about in a great deal of suet."

Perhaps for the first time, Churchill was conscious of the horrors as well as the glory of war. After the charge, the Lancers' wounded began to come in: "a succession of grisly apparitions; horses spouting blood, struggling on three legs, men staggering on foot, men bleeding from terrible wounds, fish-hook spears stuck right through them, arms and faces cut to pieces, bowels protruding, men gasping, crying, collapsing, expiring." Speculating on the shoddiness of war, he wrote, "You cannot gild it." Yet in a sense he himself was to be among its greatest gilders.

Churchill now felt he had learned all he could from war. He sent in his Army papers in 1899, despite the pleasant life he was now enjoying in India. He had played for the 4th Hussars when they won the Inter-Regimental Polo Tournament. Using almost the same metaphor as before, he had now definitely resolved to "beat my sword into a paper cutter and my sabretache into an election address."

He left the Army having learned two new things about people. First, the stoicism of the common soldier. Having asked his second sergeant whether he had enjoyed the charge, Churchill got the reply, "Well, I don't exactly say I enjoyed it Sir, but I think I'll get more used to it next time."

Second, the peculiar strength of some great men. The Mahdi ("Chosen One"), who had destroyed Gordon, had suffered like Churchill himself from a lonely childhood. "Solitary trees," commented Churchill in *The River War*, "if they grow at all grow strong."

Churchill felt himself at 24 to be a "loner" and a "chosen one." How strong would Churchill himself grow?

His first attempt to grow strong in the political field was not a resounding success. As one of the Lancer heroes from Omdurman, he was sought by Conservative associations anxious to sign him

POPPERFOTO

POPPERFOTO

Facing page: Top, a
Boer Commando. The Boers
were tough, fast-moving,
and excellent marksmen.
Bottom, a Boer gun being
hauled through the stark
and open terrain in which
much of the war was
fought.

on as their candidate. He stood for Parliament in the Lancashire
cotton town of Oldham in a by-election, but lost (July 6, 1899).
Three months later this political interlude was temporarily forgotten in another military adventure, the most exciting of Churchill's life.

By the autumn of 1899 war had broken out between Britain
and the Boer Republics in South Africa. Immediately, the *Daily
Mail* was bidding for Churchill's services as war correspondent.
True to his "pusher" motto, he promptly approached the *Morning
Post,* who overbid the *Mail* with a lavish offer of £250 a month
plus expenses. On October 14, he sailed for South Africa. His
year had opened with unusually pessimistic thoughts from India.
"What an awful thing it will be if I don't come off." Now he was
to "come off" in a big way—after very nearly coming to grief.

His adventure began in typical Churchillian fashion. On arriving at the Cape, he caught the very last train which would enable him to make a short cut to the Natal front. It seemed a good
omen. "I shall believe I am to be preserved," he wrote jubilantly,
"for future things." He had in fact gained several days on all
other war correspondents—only to lose them in a spectacular
manner, and then to regain his advantage even more decisively.

On November 15, an armoured train on which he was travelling between Estcourt and Frere was ambushed by the Boers and
three cars derailed. Churchill volunteered to organise the removal
of a car which was blocking the line, while the British soldiers
kept down enemy fire. He was successful, freeing the engine just
in time for it to return with the wounded to Estcourt. But Churchill and 51 others were captured by the Boers. Nevertheless, his
exertions and dynamic personality had won him unstinted praise
from his comrades. One man said his presence had been worth 50
men. It was even said that if he had been a soldier at the time instead of a war correspondent, he would have been awarded the
Victoria Cross—"For Valour"—always the honour he coveted most.
After being hit by a shell, the engine-driver had groaned, "I am
finished." "Buck up a bit," exhorted the indomitable Churchill, "I
will stick to you." The dialogue might have been an impromptu
rehearsal for events 40 years later.

Churchill, unarmed, had been captured by one of the tall
Boers, wearing their habitual "flapping clothes, with slouch,
storm-driven hats." These hats impressed Churchill, as did the
"wild" figure of his captor, whom he later understood to be the
famous Boer general, Louis Botha himself. (This was unlikely,
though Botha may have interrogated him.) Three days later, he

POPPERFOTO

*Churchill as a prisoner
of the Boers at Pretoria,
1899.*

31

THE MANSELL COLLECTION

*Churchill escapes.
A Boer on the horizon, a
vulture close by. "My sole
companion was a gigantic
vulture, who manifested
an extravagant interest in
my condition, and made
hideous and ominous
gurglings."*

was writing philosophically to his mother from the prison camp at Pretoria: "After all this is a new experience . . . ."

New experience or not, it was one which Churchill's temperament forbade him to endure for long. In his own graphic words, the hours crawled by like "paralytic centipedes." He spent his birthday "in durance vile," lamenting the waste of precious days. "I am 25 today—it is terrible to think how little time remains." Churchill, still obsessed with his father, believed that his own life would be equally brief and must therefore be equally meteoric. He could not wait for the eventual order of release. Only one thing would cause him to "buck up a bit"—a plan of escape.

Thanks to his lucky star—or so Churchill was convinced—he made a thrilling escape on December 12, 1899, beginning with an artless vault over the latrine wall. The stars in the shape of the constellation Orion guided Churchill from Pretoria towards a railway line where he jumped a train, riding on the couplings to Witbank. There his own star took over, for—in the midst of all those Boers—it led him to the house of an *English* manager of the Transvaal Collieries, who concealed him in the mine until the manager and his friends could concert Churchill's final exit. Hidden on a freight train among bales of wool, he made his way to Lourenço Marques in Portuguese East Africa and from there went by steamer to Durban.

Churchill entered Durban amid a tumult of applause. He had had a price of £25 on his head. Like Byron, he could have said: "I awoke one morning and found myself famous." Before returning to his duties as war correspondent, he dined with the Governor of Natal. Sir Redvers Buller, commander of British forces in South Africa, was dazzled by young Churchill's panache. "He really is a fine fellow . . . . I wish he was leading regular troops instead of writing for a rotten paper." A naval commander who also met Churchill predicted that he would one day be Prime Minister: "You possess the two necessary qualifications genius and plod." Churchill would surely have added luck. "I have a good belief," he wrote, "that I am to be of some use and therefore to be spared."

He continued to report the war until the British entry into Pretoria, where he and his cousin, now Duke of Marlborough, galloped ahead of the army, Churchill personally tearing down the Boer flag over the prison.

He returned to England on July 20, 1900, in time to stand for Parliament in the "Khaki Election" that autumn. His fame had gone before him. He wrote to Jack: "I have greatly improved my

POPPERFOTO

position in England by the events of the last year." But unjust notoriety was also to be his meed. Having eluded his Boer adversaries, he was to be pursued by his British enemies with the mischievous lie that he had broken parole by escaping from the prison. Despite a law suit and apology in 1912, the accusation was casually repeated during a television "tribute" for his 90th birthday.

In his second Oldham campaign, Churchill nevertheless was a star attraction. During his first speech, he mentioned by name, among others, a miner from Oldham who had helped him to escape capture by the Boers. "His wife's in the gallery!" shouted the joyful audience. Her husband had whispered to Churchill at Witbank before winding him down the mine, "They'll all vote for you next time!" At least enough of them did so on polling day, October 1, 1900, to give Churchill a majority of 222.

Since a seat in Parliament imposed a financial burden on its holder, Churchill now bent himself to adding to the modest earnings from his literary endeavours. A series of lecture tours, including a trip to Canada and the United States, brought his past two years' earnings to a grand total of £10,000. Mark Twain had taken the chair for him in New York, introducing him as an Englishman by his father and an American by his mother, "no doubt a blend that makes the perfect man." Then he signed his own works for Churchill, beginning with the advice, "To be good is noble; to teach others how to be good is nobler, and no trouble." The date of Mark Twain's inscription was January 22, 1901. On that day Queen Victoria died.

The Boers put £25 on his head.

POPPERFOTO

After his escape, Churchill rejoined the Army in the South African Light Horse as a lieutenant. From his Army career, Churchill learned discipline and comradeship, perhaps as valuable as a university training. "Still, one would like to have both."

33

The Glow-Worm

We are all worms.
But I do believe that
I am a glow-worm.
CHURCHILL TO
VIOLET ASQUITH, 1906

POPPERFOTO

Churchill sailed for England on February 2 while the old Queen was being buried. But though the Victorian age was buried with her, Winston was to fight for another four years under an old banner—that of his father. The brilliant Lord Randolph had risen to be a Tory minister. He had resigned his office on the issue of economy and was never invited back. Now the son also challenged his Conservative colleagues on economy, helping to form for this purpose a latter-day "Fourth Party" named "The Hooligans." It was sometimes spelled "Hughligans," after Lord Hugh Cecil, a co-founder. The membership was aristocratic, embellished however by Ian Malcolm, son-in-law of Lily Langtry, who won the Prince of Wales's devotion through her sheer beauty. One of the Hooligans' bizarre achievements was to "loiter out" a Tory bill (instead of filibustering) by declining to leave the "No" Lobby until the time allotted for debate and disposition of the bill had expired.

A split rapidly developed between Churchill and his official party. They abhorred his verbal violence; he gave up hope of ever converting them to something like Tory Democracy, his father's ideal. At first he dreamed of a middle way—of a new, centre, party—free both from "the sordid selfishness" of Toryism and "the blind appetites of the Radical masses." But soon he was writing: "I hate the Tory party . . . . I am an English Liberal." On May 31, 1904, he crossed the floor of the House of Commons.

Facing page: The "Siege of Sidney Street," 1910, only one of many controversial activities in which Churchill engaged during his early political career. Churchill, to the fore, wearing a top hat, couldn't resist directing operations on the spot.

By becoming a Liberal in time for the dramatic 1906 election, Churchill had "taken at the flood," in Shakespeare's words, one of the mightiest radical tides of history, which did indeed lead him on to greatness. He stood as Liberal candidate to represent North-West Manchester, a great Free Trade centre. The Conservatives were in disarray over their new policy of Protection, the imposition of trade tariffs. "I have nailed my colours to the fence," declared one bemused Tory. Churchill always nailed his colours to the mast, though not always the same mast. The Tories were swept away, retaining only 157 seats in a House of 670.

From being a stellar attraction in the Khaki Election of 1900, Churchill had become the rising sun of 1906. Only a year after crossing the floor, he was peppering the Tories with Liberal shot, as to the manner born: "Corruption at home, aggression to cover it up abroad ... sentiment by the bucketful, patriotism by the Imperial pint, the open hand at the public exchequer, the open door at the public house, dear food for the million, cheap labour for the millionaire. . . ."

Economic issues presented no problem. Had he not at 21 conducted "great discussions with Mr. Bourke Cockran in New York, on every conceivable subject, from economics to yacht racing"? Now at 31 he "learned" economics again, this time in eight weeks from a Treasury official, supplemented by studying six printed volumes. Girded in this possibly inadequate armour, "I found no difficulty in doing the rest myself."

Simultaneously with the election campaign, he published his famous biography of his father, *Lord Randolph Churchill*. Interest in the book was such that Churchill was paid £8,000 for publishing rights. Critics praised—and were amazed by—the author's "maturity of judgement, levelheadedness and discretion." This book and its successors were virtually all dictated by him, so that Churchill lived, as he said, "from mouth to hand."

Sir Henry Campbell-Bannerman, the Liberal Prime Minister, encouraged this brilliant young convert to his party by naming him Under-Secretary of State for the Colonies. When the Liberals were denounced for referring to coolie labour in South Africa as "Chinese Slavery," Churchill admitted that his party had been guilty of a "terminological inexactitude"—one of his happiest phrases. In 1907, he was created a Privy Councillor, an indication that he was graduating from politician to statesman.

In 1908, H. H. Asquith succeeded Campbell-Bannerman as Prime Minister and appointed Churchill to the Cabinet as President of the Board of Trade. In those days, a new Minister had to defend his seat in a by-election. Churchill lost North-West Manchester. The Tory press chanted with joy: "Winston Churchill is out, OUT, O U T!" But he was immediately invited to contest the safe, working-class—and therefore Liberal—seat of Dundee, another piece of his legendary luck.

Churchill's oratory was now established: the dazzling (sometimes overprepared) invective delivered with a slight lisp, the "brooding forehead" but infinitely mobile expression—"His was a face that could not keep a secret." The poet and writer Wilfred Scawen Blunt, one of the most colourful personalities of the period, found Churchill endowed with all his father's "gaminerie" and plainspokenness, but with literary ability added. "He interested me immensely."

Others also, both women and men, were finding him interesting, even compelling.

Winston's grandmother, Duchess Fanny, made a shrewd comment on the one novel he wrote, *Savrola:* "It is clear you have not yet attained a knowledge of Women—and it is evident you have (I am thankful to see) no experience of Love!" At this date, 1898, Duchess Fanny was right. Her grandson's first love was the beautiful Pamela Plowden, whom he met in India; but though they became unofficially engaged she seemed to have felt that marriage would be a mistake. She did Winston two good turns. She married the Earl of Lytton instead of him, and gave Winston's devoted secretary, Eddie Marsh, a unique guideline on his employer's character: "The first time you meet Winston you see all his faults, and the rest of your life you spend in discovering his virtues."

Winston tried to persuade two other women, heiress Muriel Wilson and actress Ethel Barrymore, that his virtues were irresistible. Wisely, they refused him, though remaining lifelong friends. The fact was that he was not then ready for marriage. By 1908, however, he had got to know Clementine Hozier, as lovely as Pamela and "interested" in him, despite his having stared at her in gauche silence on the occasion of their first meeting, four years earlier. Though Churchill sometimes managed to ask a girl her age, he always said he had no small talk. He might have admitted that he often appeared like a combination of Wellington and Peel—"I have no small talk," said the Iron Duke, "and Peel has no manners." Daughter of Lady Randolph's friend, Lady Blanche Hozier, Clementine was also goddaughter of Winston's uncle Jack Leslie. They were married on September 12, 1908, and in Winston's convincing words, "lived happily ever afterwards." They were to sign their early love letters with the symbolic drawings of a cat and dog respectively, "Pug" Winston thus rightly claiming the canine virtue of faithfulness and attributing to his "Pussy-Kat" every feline and other grace. Their first "Puppy-Kitten" (which turned out to be Diana) was born in 1909, followed in 1911 by their son Randolph, known before birth for some unremembered reason as the "Chum Bolly."

Winston's best man had been Lord Hugh Cecil, described by him as a real Tory out of the seventeenth century, but "equipped

POPPERFOTO

Churchill became a Liberal in 1904. His "brooding forehead" and spotted bow tie were already becoming well known.

TERENCE LE GOUBIN/CAMERA PRESS LTD.

Admitting that the Liberal accusation of Chinese slavery in South Africa was a "terminological inexactitude."

SYNDICATION INTERNATIONAL

Daily Mirror

THE MORNING JOURNAL WITH THE SECOND LARGEST NET SALE.

No. 1,414.   Registered at the G. P. O. as a Newspaper   MONDAY, MAY 11, 1908.   One Halfpenny.

ASK FOR the Special Extra

BEAUTY NUMBER

of the "DAILY MIRROR."

PRICE ONE PENNY.

NOW ON SALE.

MR. WINSTON CHURCHILL FINDS "A SAFE SEAT" AT LAST: REJECTED IN MANCHESTER, HE IS ELECTED M.P. FOR DUNDEE.

Amid scenes of tremendous excitement Mr. Winston Churchill was declared member for Dundee on Saturday night, having polled 2,709 more votes than Sir George Baxter, the Unionist candidate. The Liberal majority, however, is practically only half what it was at the general election, when Mr. E. Robertson polled 5,411 more votes than the Unionist. In the photograph Mr. Churchill is acknowledging the cheers of his supporters.—[*Daily Mirror* photograph.]

Elected Liberal Member of Parliament for Dundee in 1908. In this campaign he coined one of his epigrams: "The British Constitution is mainly British common sense."

MADAME TUSSAUD'S LTD.

The Sketch

No. 816.—Vol. LXIII.   WEDNESDAY, SEPTEMBER 16, 1908.   SIXPENCE.

Fame at last! A wax model at Madame Tussaud's.

REALLY CELEBRATED AT LAST! MR. WINSTON CHURCHILL IN WAX, AT MADAME TUSSAUD'S.

Photograph specially taken for "The Sketch" by Tofield.

POPPERFOTO

With his wife-to-be, Clementine Hozier, a week before their marriage.

with every modern convenience." "Linky" Cecil, however, was not typical of Winston's friends, who tended to be men of robust, full-blooded temperament, radiating exceptional charm. Young Randolph's godfather was F. E. Smith, later the incomparable Lord Birkenhead and Winston's family and political friend for life. In 1911, Winston met the Canadian Max Aitken who, as the future Lord Beaverbrook, was to represent for Winston the New World come to restore the balance of the Old, as well as the best of holiday companions. Five years earlier, he had formed a close friendship with the Prime Minister's daughter, Violet Asquith. To her, in her *Winston Churchill As I Knew Him,** we owe many remarkable insights and anecdotes, high among them his moment of self-revelation during their first encounter. Having confided to her his curious obsession that he would die young, Winston produced the oracular gem: "We are all worms. But I do believe that I am a glow-worm."

The Liberal landslide of 1906 had not persuaded satirical poet Hilaire Belloc that things were really going to be any different. He wrote his oft-quoted epigram:

> *The accursed power that stands on privilege*
> *And goes with women and champagne and bridge*
> *Broke, and democracy resumed her reign*
> *Which goes with bridge and women and champagne.*

* Published in the United States under the title *Winston Churchill: An Intimate Portrait.*

40

Many Tories, however, saw in the election results a harbinger of drastic social changes. They were right.

As President of the Board of Trade and representing in Parliament the working-class district of Dundee, Churchill plunged into social reform. The Trade Boards Act against sweated labour was his work, as also the introduction of Labour Exchanges. In the latter he was encouraged by the formidable socialist crusader, Beatrice Webb. Winston had begun by finding her charms less than irresistible. "I refuse to be shut up in a soup kitchen with Mrs. Sidney Webb." Later he recanted, characteristically recognising a good thing when he saw it. His initial plans for social insurance were in due course taken over by David Lloyd George. But not before Churchill had told Harold Wilson's father that he would have the word "Insure" written over every front door in the land.

Lloyd George was Chancellor of the Exchequer in Asquith's dynamic Government. His Welsh magic would always, to the end of his picaresque life, fascinate Churchill. In 1909, Lloyd George introduced his "People's Budget," only to find it vetoed by an unregenerate House of Lords. A "Peers v. People" campaign thereupon developed with the velocity of a whirlwind, on which Lloyd George rode triumphant, hurling thunderbolts at dukes. "A fully-equipped duke costs as much to keep up as two Dreadnoughts . . . ." Mindful of his dear cousin Charles ("Sunny") Marlborough, Winston followed with a playful plea for their graces: "Do not let us be too hard on them. It is poor sport—almost like teasing goldfish. . . ." The real fight, said Churchill, would be between Parliament and the mass of backwoods peers, between "a representative assembly and a miserable minority of titled persons who represent nobody, who are responsible to nobody and who only scurry up to London to vote in their party interests, their class interests and in their own interests."

The budget was passed by a temporarily cowed House of Lords. But the next item on the Liberals' programme, Home Rule for Ireland, was still threatened by the Lords' veto. Finally, in 1911, during the hottest August, physically and emotionally, within memory, the hereditary Chamber had its powers docked by the Parliament Act. Only the King's pledge to create, if necessary, enough Liberal peers to outnumber the diehards had got the Bill through.

Occupying the key post of Home Secretary since 1910, Churchill meanwhile was having his clashes with the many elements of this agitated period—from the King to the suffragettes. One phrase in the Home Secretary's nightly letters to the monarch

A later photograph of Mrs. Churchill.

THE PRESS ASSOCIATION LTD.

Walking to the House of Commons with the famous lowering look.

was deeply resented by George V: "It must not however be forgotten," wrote Churchill to his sovereign, "that there are idlers and wastrels at both ends of the social scale...." This remark the King considered "quite superfluous" and Churchill's views "very socialistic."

The strikers of Tonypandy in 1910 and of Llanelly the next year, on the contrary, branded Churchill a violent reactionary. He had ordered troops to stand by in support of the police, and at Llanelly four rioters were killed. There were no Tonypandy "martyrs." (The Tolpuddle martyrs were a group of Dorset labourers of the previous century whose attempt to form a union resulted in a notoriously vicious reaction by the authorities.) Nevertheless, the overall circumstances, and perhaps the verbal similarity between Tolpuddle and Tonypandy, long estranged him from the organised workers.

Churchill himself facilitated the process by his rash participation in the "Siege of Sidney Street." An armed gang was trapped by the police in London's East End. Soon troops from the Tower, the fire brigade, and, alas, Churchill himself were all on the scene. He had not been able to resist the fun of "directing operations," as the music halls put it. For this he was heartily booed.

He had revived the forgotten word "henpecking" to describe the behaviour of the suffragettes at his meetings. The word stuck. So did his connection with "Black Friday" (November 18, 1910) and with the "Battle of Downing Street" (November 22). On the first occasion, the police had manhandled the suffragettes; and on the second, Churchill had the much respected Mrs. Cobden-Sanderson removed with the curt order, "Take that woman away." Four days later, he himself was horse-whipped in the corridor of a train by a male student—"Take that you dirty cur." Yet he favoured the vote for women—at least for womanly women. Fifty years later, when founding Churchill College, it was Churchill personally who was the first to suggest that women be admitted.

Amid this welter of controversial events, it is sometimes forgotten that Churchill made a genuine mark on penal reform. His short term as Home Secretary gave him little time to get reforms on the Statute Book. But his own incarceration by the Boers inspired him to do what he could, through encouraging lectures and other cultural activities, to make prison hours—those "paralytic centipedes"—pass more quickly.

In a few short years, Churchill had gone from political newcomer to Cabinet member, an impressive beginning. But while his association with the social programmes of the Liberals made him even more odious to Conservatives, his activities as Home Secretary brought him under fire from the Radical wing of the Liberal party. A few years and many controversies later, he would find himself a political outcast.

POPPERFOTO

Suffragettes in action. As Home Secretary, Churchill was one of their targets.

During the Agadir crisis of July, 1911, Churchill found himself sitting on an "idle hill of summer" in Somerset, haunted by Housman's *A Shropshire Lad:*

> *Far and near and low and louder*
> *On the roads of earth go by,*
> *Dear to friends and food for powder,*
> *Soldiers marching, all to die.*

The crisis had been caused by the arrival of a German gunboat, the *Panther,* at the Moroccan port of Agadir. In the taut state of international relations, it was seen as a sinister German attempt to create a new sphere of influence. In the end, after a certain amount of sabre-rattling on both sides, the *Panther* withdrew. But Churchill had glimpsed Armageddon; with characteristic exuberance, he began to steep himself in military and naval matters and to circulate memoranda warning of the dangers of war.

Friction between the Admiralty and the War Office, meanwhile, convinced Asquith to make a change at the Admiralty. While spending a September weekend with the Asquiths, Churchill pressed Asquith to give him the post of First Lord.

"Will you come out for a walk with me—at once?" Winston asked Violet Asquith breathlessly.

"You don't want tea?"

"No, I don't want tea. I don't want tea—I don't want anything —anything in the world. Your father has just offered me the Admiralty."

Churchill, in Privy Councillor's uniform, going to Buckingham Palace in a taxi. Official cars were not yet provided, and Churchill did not own a car until 1923.

POPPERFOTO/CONWAY PICTURE LIBRARY

POPPERFOTO/PUNCH

Prime Minister Asquith teases his notorious First Lord of the Admiralty on board the yacht Enchantress, *1913. Churchill: "Any home news?" Asquith: "How can there be with you here?"*

Churchill had got what he wanted: responsibility and power—the power to defend his threatened country with its most potent arm, the Navy.

Overboard went his old shibboleths on economy in defence, inherited from his father. They were fatally at variance with "the deep tides of destiny," as he now saw them. Henceforth he was to do battle for vastly increased naval budgets. His object was three-fold: to equip the Navy with 15-inch guns, to create a Fast Division, and to convert the Fleet from coal to oil. He also aimed at reforms on the lower deck. After a titanic struggle, he got his funds in 1913, with the proviso that they should be cut back the following year. In 1914 Armageddon supervened.

His obsession with the Navy caused some friendly criticism beyond and beside the innate Liberal distaste for expenditure on armaments. "You have become a water creature," expostulated Lloyd George. "You think we all live in the sea.... You forget that most of us live on land." But what some people saw as an obsession could equally well have been considered God-given concentration.

Throughout the struggle for a modern fleet, Churchill was superlatively served by his growing eloquence in Parliament. The Admiralty, he found, was split from top to bottom by personal antagonisms, reflected in disputes over policy. He pilloried his opponent, a retired admiral, now M.P. for Portsmouth: "Lord

Charles Beresford can best be described as one of those orators who, before they get up, do not know what they are going to say, when they are speaking do not know what they are saying, and when they have sat down, do not know what they have said." His enemies in the Admiralty retorted that he was dictatorial or, alternatively, too fond of discussing policy with junior officers.

———————

Churchill's exhilarated concern for Britain's naval bulwark brought him into sharp collision with Ulster (Protestant Northern Ireland). In his view, Ireland could be a safe neighbour only if pacified by self-government, or Home Rule. But Ulster Unionists, still inflamed by his own father's dangerous slogan—"Ulster will fight and Ulster will be right"—were resolved to risk anything rather than be ruled in domestic affairs from Catholic Dublin.

While standing fast by Home Rule, the First Lord worked behind the scenes for a compromise settlement. But the journey of the Home Rule Bill towards the Statute Book in 1914 stirred the Ulster Protestants to revolutionary resistance. On March 14, Churchill denounced them in scathing terms: "They uphold all law except the law they choose to break. . . . The veto of violence

Lord Fisher and Churchill leaving an Imperial Defence Committee meeting in 1913. Fisher inspired some of Churchill's naval reforms.

THE PRESS ASSOCIATION LTD.

has replaced the veto of privilege." He warned them the Government would take firm action. Five days later, on his own initiative, he signalled the 3rd Battle Squadron to proceed to Lamlash in Scotland, 75 miles from Belfast. Asquith countermanded these orders as soon as he learned of them, but too late to keep them from being made public. This, coupled with the mass resignation of officers at the Curragh camp near Dublin (though the officers were soon reinstated), unleashed a storm of criticism in Parliament. Churchill was cast as a major villain in a Government "plot" to provoke Ulster to violence.

In fact, a mightier "veto of violence," which was to overshadow the Irish problem, waited in the wings. At the Admiralty, Churchill had concentrated on maintaining superiority over the expanding German Grand Fleet. He now felt confidence in Britain's strength at sea—and in the air, for he had brought into being the new Royal Naval Air Service. He even learned to fly himself, an expertise which caused his wife so much alarm, however, that he desisted, apologising to Clemmie: "My darling one, I will not fly any more until at any rate you have recovered from your kitten [Sarah]. . . . I am sure my nerve, my spirits & my virtue were all improved by it. But at your expense my poor pussy cat! I am so sorry."

"The Nelson Touch" (below, left) satirises Churchill's battle for a vastly increased naval budget. His "Sea-Change" from demanding economy in defence forced even Conservative party opponents to admire his naval ardour. The "Tory Chorus" sings, "You've made me love you. I didn't want to do it."

A SEA-CHANGE.

SYNDICATION INTERNATIONAL

The assassination of Archduke Franz-Ferdinand of Austria-Hungary on June 28, 1914, occasioned little immediate change in the European diplomatic scene. By the last week in July, however, events were rushing to a climax. On July 24, Austria presented its ultimatum to Serbia. The British fleet at that time was about to disperse after a test mobilisation. But on the 26th, Admiral Prince Louis of Battenberg, First Sea Lord, heard of Austria's intransigent attitude following Serbia's conciliatory response to the ultimatum. He took his famous initiative—"postponing" (to quote Asquith's word to the King) dispersal of the fleet. Churchill, at Cromer with his "kittens," immediately approved this crucial measure and hurried back to London.

In three months' time, when Battenberg, tragically, had to resign, Churchill offered splendid consolation: "The first step which secured the timely concentration of the Fleet was taken by you."

In ten months' time, when Churchill in turn was removed, Kitchener was to do the same for him. "Well, there is one thing at any rate they cannot take from you. The Fleet was ready."

Churchill with Kaiser Wilhelm II at military manoeuvres in Germany.

The First World Crisis

*My God! This,
this is
living History.*
CHURCHILL TO MARGOT ASQUITH,
JANUARY, 1915

POPPERFOTO

Churchill entered the fray with a lift of the heart. That was his temperament. Events and situations were more than tonics, they were intoxicants. In the week before war broke out, he had written to Clemmie. "My darling one & beautiful," he began. "Everything tends towards catastrophe & collapse. I am interested, geared up & happy. Is it not horrible to be built like that?"

He was, of course, not built entirely "like that." Five years earlier, after watching the German manoeuvres, he had shown his wife the other side of his nature: "Much as war attracts me & fascinates my mind with its tremendous situations—I feel more deeply every year . . . what vile & wicked folly & barbarism it all is. . . ." But in 1914 he responded overwhelmingly to the challenge and overlooked the vileness.

Lloyd George, himself the embodiment of dynamic force, was half amused, half amazed by the First Lord's hyperactivity. He was to paint a gay picture of Winston's irruption into No. 10 Downing Street at 11:15 p.m. on August 4, 1914, after giving the signal "Commence hostilities" to the Fleet. "Winston dashed into the room, radiant, his face bright, his manner keen, one word pouring out on another how he was going to send telegrams to the Mediterranean, the North Sea, and God knows where. You could see he was a really happy man."

The first event of the naval war, however, was a disaster—the sinking of the light cruiser *Amphion* by a German mine. Next, the German warships *Goeben* and *Breslau* eluded the Admiralty's vigilance and escaped through the Dardanelles to Constantinople. By the fourth week in August, the Allies were hotly engaged in Belgium and not to their advantage. Churchill telegraphed the words "disappointing" and "serious" to Admiral Jellicoe waiting at Scapa Flow for the German High Seas Fleet to come out. He wrote the same to his brother, Jack, adding to the latter, "Unless we win, I do not want to live any more. But win we will."

The question was how to win. Churchill's fertile mind was working overtime. He sounded out the Russians on a sea invasion of Germany, with British naval cooperation; but he got a dusty

Facing page: The end of the greatest war the world had ever known; proclamation of the Armistice to troops in France, 1918.

51

answer. Solzhenitsyn's *August 1914* reiterates Russia's unfitness to carry out even the most obvious strategy. Then he advocated compulsory service. Kitchener, however, now Secretary of State for War, was against this innovation. Not Churchill's brain-wave but Kitchener's own recruiting posters were expected to fill the ranks. The author remembers seeing as a child Kitchener's huge portrait on the curved wall of a London Underground station. As you moved up and down the subway platform, the eyes and forefinger —almost the voice—followed you: "Your Country Needs *You!*"

Churchill's first acceptable idea was to send 3,000 Marines to Ostend on the Belgian coast on August 26. They were brought home within the week, but they had, as he hoped, alarmed the Germans. As if fortune had begun to smile, a naval victory followed two days later in the Heligoland Bight. Three German cruisers were sunk and three damaged. At a subsequent Guildhall Banquet, there were insistent calls for "Churchill! Churchill! Churchill! We want Churchill!" It seemed they could not have enough of him. He spoke to them in language which had come to him from Gibbon and Pitt and Macaulay but was now wholly his own: "You have only to endure to conquer. You have only to persevere to save yourselves, and to save all those who rely upon you. You have only to go right on, and at the end of the road, be it short or long, victory and honour will be found!"

Endure, persevere, save, conquer . . . . He was already collecting the armoury of words which, a quarter of a century later, was to save the Western World and all those who relied upon it.

Yet another military operation had been initiated on the very day before the Guildhall Banquet, September 3. It was originally Kitchener's idea; but once lodged in Churchill's brain it proliferated. And as the idea developed, so did a whisper grow into a murmur and then into a loud protest that Churchill was going too far.

Its critics called the operation the Dunkirk Circus. Kitchener had requested Churchill to take over the entire air defence of Britain against zeppelin raids. Churchill had already ordered the establishment of a Royal Naval Air Service base at Dunkirk, on the northern coast of France. Activities at the base quickly expanded, finally leading to the production of armoured cars which in turn, some years later, would spawn tanks. Churchill's contribution to the invention and development of the tank should never be forgotten. "Thus the Air was the first cause that took us to Dun-

IMPERIAL WAR MUSEUM

Mr Churchill with his humble duty to Your Majesty has the honour to submit the accompanying photographs of the new 15" howitzer.

Twelve of these guns are under construction. The first two are ready, and will be shipped to France this week, where it is proposed that they should come into action next Thursday. Two more will follow at the end of the month, and the remainder at regular intervals. There is sufficient ammunition for the early firings, and increasing quantities will be steadily forthcoming.

The building of these guns, from the designs and under the supervision of Rear Admiral Bacon, constitutes a record in production, having been entirely carried out since the war began. The proof firings exceeded in excellence all previous estimates – 11,000 yards, being *Winston Spencer Churchill*

A letter sent to King George V in February, 1915, about the new howitzer, another of Churchill's many interests.

kirk," wrote Churchill in *The World Crisis*. "The armoured car was the child of the air; and the Tank its grandchild." Then why the opprobrious term "Circus" for the valuable operations at Dunkirk?

This was mainly due to Churchill's own sense of the dramatic. He was always hopping across the Channel, having his Dunkirk "weekends" with his young pilots—among them several who had taught him to fly. (Perhaps these were in a sense the very first of the "few.") While he was at Dunkirk, his work at the Admiralty had to be supervised by others, notably the Prime Minister and First Sea Lord. The former would speak impatiently of Winston's "little army." The latter, as we shall see, was having his own troubles. But Dunkirk would surely never have had such angry critics but for what followed.

POPPERFOTO

*A sign of Churchill's
interest in flying—and of
his intrepid nature.*

In mid-September, Winston was writing cheerfully to a friend, "The days pass in an unbroken succession of events & decisions." In fact, the big events were not happening on the high seas or in the air, but on the Western Front, where the Battle of the Marne had held the German advance. The Navy was still waiting impatiently for the German fleet to fight. Thinking to relieve their frustration, Churchill said that if the Germans did not come out they would be "dug out like rats in a hole." Not only did such language make a bad impression on the Senior Service, but on the following day three British ships were sunk near the Dogger Bank. On top of this came the Antwerp operation.

The Antwerp story lasted only from October 2–10, 1914. Nevertheless, it added substantially to Churchill's slide from popularity. On the 2nd, Asquith had left London for Cardiff. Churchill was on his way to Dover by special train. He was suddenly recalled to London by Kitchener and Foreign Secretary Sir Edward Grey with the grim news that the Belgians intended to evacuate the port of Antwerp the next morning. At Kitchener's request, Churchill immediately turned round and set off again, this time for Antwerp. It was after midnight. His orders were to persuade the Belgians, encouraged by an offer of a brigade of Marines, to hold on. The subsequent report that Churchill launched the Antwerp mission off his own bat is therefore untrue.

In Antwerp on the 3rd, Churchill was highly successful; the Belgians decided to "buck up a bit." Churchill, having asked Kitchener and Grey to confirm the offer of naval brigades, in effect took over control of the city. But the temptation to go further proved irresistible. The next day, instead of returning to London as expected, he telegraphed Asquith, proposing to resign from the Admiralty and assume formal military command at Antwerp.

There were already several major generals in Antwerp. We remember what Wellington said when he was in danger of being superseded in his command: "We want no major generals in Mysore!" But at least Wellington's rival was of his own rank. They wanted no new major general in Antwerp who was only an ex-lieutenant of hussars. Asquith recorded that Churchill's offer to the Cabinet was greeted with "Homeric" laughter.

The public did not laugh when the Belgians surrendered on October 10 and many men of the naval brigades, including young recruits, were lost. To his surprise, Churchill was widely criticised. Nevertheless, Cabinet colleagues welcomed him back as a hero, Asquith commenting on his dash of genius—that "zigzag streak of lightning in the brain." Though the public knew only that the fall of the city had occurred just days after Churchill's arrival there, Antwerp's lengthened defence, inspired by him, had been far from fruitless. Those few days "applied a brake to the German advance," according to the great military historian Sir Basil Liddell Hart, "that just stopped their second attempt to gain a decision in the West."

The Antwerp episode may be rounded off by a vignette of Churchill painted by an Italian war correspondent. It described a man, still young, wearing a yachting cap and peacefully smoking a large cigar as he watched the progress of the battle under a "fearful" rain of shrapnel. Not a Minister in the whole of Europe, thought the Italian, could have behaved with such sangfroid. "He smiled, and looked quite satisfied."

Churchill might not have looked so satisfied had he known what was in store for him over the next year. At the end of October, Prince Louis of Battenberg, the loyal and outstandingly able First Sea Lord (chief professional adviser to the Admiralty), who had given his whole life to the British Navy, was scuppered. A shameful campaign against his German birth had been whipped up by certain organs of the press. Attacked publicly as the "Germ-hun" in the popular magazine *John Bull* and assailed by poison-pen

POPPERFOTO/PUNCH

"Lord Fisher comes aboard." To replace Prince Louis of Battenberg as First Sea Lord, Churchill appointed "Jacky" Fisher, a popular move. There was a "magnetic mutual attraction" between them.

letters, he was also privately slandered by Churchill's old enemy Lord Charles Beresford. His health was finally affected. Realising that he had become a liability to the Service he loved, he resigned on October 29, 1914.

The severity of his loss became evident all too soon. "There is no one else suitable for the post," Churchill had said to Asquith. He was thinking of Prince Louis's ability as administrator and commander. But Richard Hough, Prince Louis's biographer, has pointed out that also essential to the smooth running of the Admiralty was the personal side of the Churchill-Battenberg partnership. "There was no one in the service with Louis's experience . . . who knew both how to tame Churchill without fighting him, encouraging him without being outraged by his excesses. The nation and the Royal Navy needed Churchill in war, and with him they needed Prince Louis as the *only* working partner." In Prince Louis's place, Churchill appointed John ("Jacky") Fisher, an admiral who, at 74, had been on the retired list since 1910. Lord Fisher was immensely popular and a technical innovator of genius. It was he who had inspired Churchill to improve the conditions and pay of naval ratings. He had once had fire in his belly and was still a fire-eater on paper. But he could not stand up to the politicians. He was no partner for Churchill.

It has been said that Churchill entered the war with two time-bombs in his luggage. One was Tory hatred for Churchill the party renegade; the other, Labour distrust for Churchill the strike-breaker. A bad external situation could set these bombs off.

By mid-October, 1914, the situation was deteriorating. Martin Gilbert, Churchill's biographer after the lamented death of his son, Randolph, has written: "Public confidence in the Navy was ebbing away." Among the causes were British losses and German escapes at sea; Churchill's involvement with the Dunkirk Circus; German seizure of Ostend and Antwerp; Churchill's alleged interference with the Sea Lords' advice; and, above all, the British Navy's failure to bring the Germans to battle.

With the return of Fisher to the Admiralty, Churchill hoped to restore public confidence. Moreover there was "a magnetic mutual attraction between these two," as Violet Asquith said. Even Fisher's amazing literary style may have fascinated the artist in Churchill. Fisher tended to write letters in exclamatory capitals, such as "LOCK the Germans up! DO SOMETHING !!!!! *We are waiting to be kicked* !!! Next kick this week! Yours F."

56

A bad "kick" had occurred immediately after Fisher's installation: the Battle of Coronel on November 1, when two British ships and 1,500 men went down. Asquith told Churchill it was "time that he bagged something, & broke some crockery." On December 8, the "crockery" was duly broken at the Battle of the Falkland Islands. Two German light cruisers and the heavy cruisers *Gneisenau* and *Scharnhorst*, the latter being the flagship of Admiral von Spee, victor of Coronel, were all sunk. The threat from the German cruisers was over. But the deadlock on the Western Front remained. In Churchill's words, there was nothing for the Allied troops but to "chew barbed wire."

In the East, on the contrary, events were moving towards catastrophe. Turkey had entered the war against the Allies in October, and Russia's position in the Caucasus had become desperate. It was imperative that some operation be mounted to take pressure off Russia.

On New Year's Day, 1915, the call to action seemed to have come. Two "pregnant" memoranda, one from Lloyd George and one from Colonel Hankey, secretary to the War Council, were circulated. Both, noted Churchill excitedly, pointed to the Near East as the true field for future operations. Churchill's mind at that precise moment had been running on a plan to relieve Russia by attacking Germany in the Baltic. But less than a month before, his focus had been Gallipoli. "His volatile mind," wrote Asquith, was set on Turkey and Bulgaria, "& he wants to organise an heroic adventure against Gallipoli and the Dardanelles . . . ."

Gallipoli was the narrow peninsula adjoining the Dardanelles, the straits which connected the Aegean with the Sea of Marmara. If a naval force could break through the Dardanelles, the end result would almost certainly be the occupation of the Turkish capital, Constantinople. Churchill had wanted Gallipoli to be attacked the very moment war was declared.

Volatile or not, Churchill did not ignore the claims of reason and logic. Much as he yearned for a campaign in Gallipoli, he could not entertain the idea of it coming off without a combined naval and military force. So when Kitchener himself approached him on that New Year's Day with a tentative proposal, Churchill was skeptical.

"Could we not, for instance," Kitchener asked, "make a demonstration at the Dardanelles?"

Not with ships alone was the burden of Churchill's reply. Churchill's tragedy was to be driven to undermine this New Year's resolution within three days.

On January 3, he was telegraphing Vice-Admiral Carden, commander of the Blockading Squadron at the Dardanelles: "Do you consider the forcing of the Dardanelles by ships alone a practical operation?" Thus the fatal words—"by ships alone"—had got on to paper.

To everyone's surprise, including Churchill and Fisher, Admiral Carden replied with a qualified "Yes." Next day, with the War Council's approval, Churchill was asking Carden for amplification. While he awaited the answer his spirits soared. "My God! This, this is living History," he exclaimed to Asquith's wife, Margot. "Why I would not be out of this glorious delicious war for anything the world could give me." Suddenly a twinge of conscience. "I say don't repeat that I said the word 'delicious'—you know what I mean."

Yet Churchill had an excellent precedent for that dangerous word. His great hero, Stonewall Jackson, had used it during the American Civil War. "Delicious excitement!" murmured Jackson to Robert E. Lee at dawn before battle. "It is well that war is so horrible—we would grow too fond of it." Churchill was later to quote Jackson's words in his *History of the English-Speaking Peoples.*

Carden's reply arrived on the 12th—to Churchill, "*the* most important telegram." In Carden's view, it would be possible to force the Dardanelles without troops in about a month, and break into the Sea of Marmara. Churchill still had doubts about the feasibility of this Near East strategy, harping on his plans for Northern Europe. But events were moving fast in the Gallipoli direction. The whole Admiralty War Group thrashed out Carden's proposals. Fisher even suggested that the *Queen Elizabeth,* newest and most powerful ship in the Fleet, should be added to the older, pre-Dreadnought, ships bound for the Dardanelles. On the 13th there was a War Council and the crucial decision was taken, with a directive to the Admiralty: "That the Admiralty should . . . prepare for a naval expedition in February to bombard and take the Gallipoli peninsula, with Constantinople as its objective."

January 13 happened to be the Russian New Year. In stirring language, Churchill sent a New Year's message to the Russian people, dedicating the audacious new plan to them. He told them that Britain's resources were "within reach" and "inexhaustible," her mind "made up." None of these things was in fact certain. The first part of the campaign was to fail precisely because resources were inadequate and out of reach. Or as Churchill might have said: "Too little and too late."

POPPERFOTO

As for Britain's mind being "made up," her First Sea Lord was changing his mind back and forth with all the querulousness of old age. During the first week in January, Fisher had tried to resign over aerial defence; the only retort to the "zepp," he held, was shooting German prisoners of war. Soon he was talking about resignation on the Dardanelles issue itself. *"I don't agree with one single step taken,"* he told Admiral Jellicoe on the 19th, and again on the 21st: "I just abominate the Dardanelles operation, unless a great change is made and it is settled to be made a military operation, with 200,000 men in conjunction with the Fleet." Churchill also, of course, would very much have preferred a combined operation. But Kitchener, the great warlord, had ruled this out.

The first "Fisher crisis" came on January 28, when the First Sea Lord sent in his resignation to the First Lord. By now Fisher had swung totally against using "ANY 'Queen Elizabeths' or ANY Battle Cruisers whatever" in the Dardanelles, a theatre of war which he did not regard as "decisive." Instead of attending the War Council that day, he would "revert to roses at Richmond"— which meant that after resigning he would have time to do the pruning in his garden.

Above, left: Prince Louis of Battenberg walks with Churchill. Prince Louis's forced resignation as First Sea Lord led to the return of Lord Fisher and subsequently to Churchill's ouster from the Government, in 1915. Churchill assuaged the political wound by serving as a soldier in France with the Royal Scots Fusiliers. Here he is in 1916, with his second-in-command, Major Sir Archibald Sinclair, who was to enter Churchill's Government during the Second World War.

POPPERFOTO

POPPERFOTO

Churchill and Asquith might now have seized the chance to prune this prickly growth from the Admiralty. Instead, Asquith forced Fisher to the Council table, and when Fisher left the table during the meeting, Kitchener brought him back. That afternoon Churchill used all his arts of rhetoric and reason upon Fisher. The old man at last crumbled. He not only accepted the necessity of the Dardanelles naval operation, but, in his own words, "I went the whole hog, *totus porcus.*"

There was a fortnight or more of steady preparation, in an atmosphere of unity and enthusiasm. Then doubts struck again, not from Fisher but from another member of the Admiralty War Group. A memo circulated on February 15 called for "a strong military force" either to assist in the bombardment or at least to follow up the silencing of the Turkish forts.

The memo had an immediate effect. The whole enterprise was transformed: suddenly it became after all a combined military and naval operation. The British 29th Division was to be sent to Gallipoli, supported by the ANZACS, or Australian and New Zealand forces. Churchill and Kitchener were thus to be in joint command.

This should have been, and was, what Churchill had always wanted. But there was one serious flaw. Kitchener's soldiers were not yet there, while Churchill's sailors were about to begin the assault. Three days later, Kitchener was finding reasons for holding back the 29th Division.

On this same day, February 19, Carden began bombarding the Turkish forts on the Dardanelles. During the next month, however, the Fleet was slowed down by bad weather and the unexpected problem of clearing mine fields.

Churchill still believed and argued that military support was indispensable. But victory seemed so much more vital that he was prepared to take the risk of going ahead without any military support, prepared to be a "guided gambler," as Violet Asquith said.

Nor could his undoubted state of euphoria have helped to convince colleagues that he believed his own arguments and warnings. Violet Asquith remembered dining with Winston and Clementine on the day that Carden announced the first bombardment. Winston suddenly said: "I think a curse should rest on me because I am so happy." How could one be happy during a cruel war? But he could not help it. "I enjoy every second I live." Later

Facing page: The Dardanelles, scene of an Allied military disaster and the cause of a major political setback for Churchill—"I'm finished, I'm done." Photos show a Turkish battery and an Allied position.

61

in the month, Violet Asquith reported: "W. speaks sanguinely of the whole thing being a picnic."

Napoleon had said the same before Waterloo . . . .

———

The first blow fell on March 18. The combined British and French naval attack on the Straits foundered in an unexpectedly vicious mine field, with the virtual loss of four ships. Churchill had expected to risk up to 12 ships but Fisher, in his heart of hearts, could not bear his precious "hardware" to be touched. As the British writer Paul Johnson said, he would have been ideal in a cold war.

On the 23rd and 27th, the Admiral in Command, now John de Robeck, insisted on full military support before advancing further. Naval gunfire alone could not completely reduce the forts. This was the moment of truth for Churchill. He had swung round to the single watchword of "Forward." Asquith and Kitchener backed him up. The glittering prize seemed within his grasp. To wait for the Army at this crucial juncture would surely be madness. One more push and the Fleet would be steaming up the Sea of Marmara towards the Golden Horn.

It was not to be. No push without the Army. In Churchill's own words, "The Admirals dug their toes in"—de Robeck, Fisher, the lot.

———

By April, three personal anxieties were nagging at Churchill. He was no longer directing the grand plan, merely supervising a subsidiary aspect of it, namely, the part to be played by the Navy in the Gallipoli landings. Again, Fisher was working up to a new burst of eccentricity. "You are just simply eaten up with the Dardanelles," he wrote petulantly to Churchill. Lastly, that implacable enemy Lord Charles Beresford and his fellow Conservatives were beginning to scent trouble in the Dardanelles. Churchill was cast for the role of scapegoat.

At last, on April 25, came the landings of 30,000 soldiers. The forces reached none of their objectives. Churchill remained hopeful that the situation would be retrieved, though he spoke of "too few men at the scene of action." Beresford and his friends, however, saw it as one man too many at the scene of decision—Churchill. When the Gallipoli ground attacks were renewed with heavy casualties on May 6 and again failed, it was clear that a crisis was imminent. Fisher, who was by now at loggerheads with

Churchill, decided once more to resign, but was just headed off by placatory gestures, including the withdrawal from Gallipoli of the *Queen Elizabeth*. Kitchener at once complained that the Navy was deserting the Army in its hour of trial. But the problems of an angry First Sea Lord and War Minister soon paled beside the debacle of a mightier titan still. The Prime Minister himself was about to face his own Furies.

On May 14, *The Times* accused the government of a shell shortage which, it said, caused the failure of the British advance in France. That same day, Asquith's mistress and confidante told him that she was going to be married. The Prime Minister was shattered. And on the next day after a meeting of the War Council, when Gallipoli had again been considered and not wound up, as Fisher was insistently demanding, the First Sea Lord resigned. This time, neither Asquith nor Churchill could dissuade him.

Fisher's resignation finished off Churchill's career at the Admiralty and precipitated a coalition. The Conservatives, under Andrew Bonar Law, seized upon the shell shortage scandal and —more important—the crisis at the Admiralty as their opportunity to press the demand for a Coalition Government. Asquith, his resolve undermined by his personal loss, was unable to resist both Bonar Law and Lloyd George, who also favoured a coalition. But formation of a coalition was only half the solution. The other half was to find a scapegoat. Asquith sent for Churchill on May 17. "I have decided to form a National Government by a coalition with the Unionists . . . . What are we to do for you?"

Nothing. The Unionists would not have Churchill in a key position at any price. As Lord Beaverbrook later reported, "Fisher was the darling of the Tory party, Churchill had become its bugbear. Was the first to go and the second to stay?" Churchill, it is true, retained a watching brief in regard to Gallipoli as Chancellor of the Duchy of Lancaster until the autumn. But he no longer possessed power or prestige. If Asquith's heart was temporarily broken, Churchill was broken in his soul.

"I'm finished. . . . I'm done," he groaned to his staunch friend Violet Asquith. He had wanted only one thing, but that thing he wanted passionately: to have a hand in winning the war. "But I can't—It's been taken from me." They might just as well have taken his life. "I thought he would die of grief," recalled his wife long afterwards. "When he left the Admiralty he thought he was finished."

It would take more than Gallipoli to finish Churchill. For one thing, there were experts who would assure him that the Gallipoli campaign was the sole brilliant strategical idea to come out of the war. Its failure was not his fault, though characteristically he had taken responsibility. For another thing, there was Kitchener's great and consoling remark: "The Fleet was ready." Whatever else Churchill's enemies took from him, they could not take the lustre of his work for the Navy between 1911 and 1914. There was also Violet Asquith, who was about to be married but always had time to encourage Churchill. Winston was lamenting that his life was at the mercy of "Fate's whirligig," when Violet interrupted him. He had a compass, she insisted, which took him to the stars. "And somewhere in that heavenly hurly-burly is your star—the one that led you in South Africa. Don't forget you've got a star."

"I shan't forget it."

Meanwhile, helpless and frustrated, he had to watch the Gallipoli tragedy unroll to its bitter end: a Turkish assault beaten off, an Anglo-French action on the Helles front, two inconclusive British general attacks, and then, from August 6–28, the great and ghastly Battle of Sulva Bay. Late in 1915, it was decided to evacuate the Gallipoli Peninsula. To everyone's surprise, it was effected with no loss of life. There might even have been rejoicings, as over an early type of "Dunkirk miracle." But the horror of the heavy casualties in August could not be forgotten. For these the obloquy fell on Churchill.

It took him 25 years completely to regain the nation's confidence. And the families of those who fought in the Gallipoli campaign never forgave him. In May, 1916, he was speaking in the House of Commons when suddenly the cry was raised, "What about the Dardanelles?" It echoed round the Chamber, in Gilbert's words, "like a widow's curse."

There will probably never be agreement about the campaign. Despite his reservations, Churchill, as we have seen, had made it peculiarly his own. Once he was involved, he always went right into a thing, "*totus porcus*," as Fisher would have said. The stakes had been prodigious: to bypass the stalemate on the Western Front and rescue the Near East and Russia. Success might have postponed or even transformed the Russian Revolution. But the stars were against.

Gallipoli was a tragedy in two parts. From January to May, 1915, it was a case of "too little and too late." As Churchill said, every week lost was about equal to the loss of a division, since the Turks were continually reinforced. From May to December, it was a case of Churchill's policy without Churchill at the helm.

A portrait by Sir William Orpen of Churchill after his resignation in 1915, christened by the artist "The Man of Misery." Churchill learned from Gallipoli a salutary lesson: not to force strategy, however brilliant, on men who did not believe in it. "Personally, I am always ready to learn," he said later, "although I do not always like being taught."

After his political fall, one of Churchill's occupations was writing. He remained a popular subject for caricature. Winston (sheathing his Sunday-paper weapon in his best Blenheim manner): "After all, some say 'the pen is mightier than the sword.'"

In his agony of frustration between May and November, 1915, Churchill had taken up painting. It began as an anodyne, a pain-killer; but it was to become, in his own language, a "pastime;" and in time almost a subsidiary profession. His mother, Jennie, wrote about Winston's painting to her sister Leonie, reporting that one of the most celebrated portrait painters of the day, Sir John Lavery, rated Winston's work highly. "Lavery says that if Winston cared to take painting up as a profession he could, but of course he uses it as an opiate."

It was an opiate which Winston had first approached with circumspection if not fear. In his enchanting essay "Painting as a Pastime," he described his first attempts to place a tiny pale blue "bean" of paint in the centre of an "affronted" snow-white canvas. Fortunately, Lady Lavery arrived at that moment and saw his hesitation. Realising that this inhibited performer was not the true Churchill, she seized his largest brush and sloshed on a great swathe of colour. He was liberated, literally at a stroke.

Once he got going, his painting was to be as romantic as the rest of his outlook on life. Violet Asquith recalled an occasion when his painting of their "flat, uneventful" surroundings included a background of dramatic mountains. In reply to her astonished questions, Winston said, "Well—I couldn't leave it quite as dull as all that." The scenery of France, Italy, Morocco, and the Vale of Kent was in time to furnish him with subjects as romantic as even he could wish.

To return to the traumas of 1915 and another revealing anecdote from Violet Asquith. He was painting one day at Herstmonceux Castle in the silence of utter concentration. (Painting was the only thing she ever saw him do in silence.) Suddenly the spell was broken by the distant sound of gunfire across the English Channel. His gloom returned. "They don't want to listen to me, or use me," he said. "They only want to keep me out."

There was one way of getting "in" again, however, which no one could bar him from. He would resign from the Government and fight on the Western Front, that desert of mud and blood where men were forced year in year out to "chew barbed wire."

———

Churchill approached his friend Sir John French, the Commander-in-Chief. French's power was not what it had been. "But it still counts for something," French told his friend. "Will you take a Brigade?" Churchill radiated enthusiasm. He would not have been Churchill otherwise. But first he must learn about trench warfare.

And to this end, another highly-placed friend, Lord Cavan, handed him over to Colonel George ("Ma") Jeffreys of the Grenadier Guards.

Ma Jeffreys was not pleased at this gift from the gods. As he conducted Churchill along the Front on the first day, there was a heavy silence. Then Jeffreys said, "I think I ought to tell you that I did not ask for you." But before the end of Churchill's training, Jeffreys had offered to make him his acting second-in-command.

Other instances of luck—or deep purpose—favoured him. While Churchill was absent from his dugout to answer a summons from the general, the dugout was blown up. He felt constrained to write about the incident afterwards: "And then . . . there came the sensation that a hand had been stretched out to move me in the nick of time from a fatal spot." At such a solemn moment, he no longer thought in terms of his own hand controlling his destiny. Another hand was guiding him. Again he had the feeling he was being preserved for a purpose—but what?

P.A. — REUTER

Diana and Randolph Churchill (centre) with their cousin Johnny Churchill, son of Winston's brother, Jack, at a wedding in 1915.

In 1916, it was apparently only to command a battalion of the 6th Royal Scots Fusiliers. The idea of a brigade had vanished when Sir Douglas Haig superseded French. But as always, Churchill threw himself into his new duties. Lice were banished and marching songs introduced. For a time he was even happy. A colleague, Captain A. D. Gibb, remembered an alarming day when "whizzbangs" were flying past their ears. Suddenly Churchill's "dreamy voice" broke in on Gibb's unpleasant reflections. "Do you like War?" Poor Gibb hated it with all his heart. "But at that and every moment," he wrote afterwards, "I believe Winston Churchill revelled in it. There was no such thing as fear in him. . . ."

Gibb was right. But the point was a subtle one. Churchill rejoiced at being *right in* a situation, up to the hilt. For a limited time he would give himself up completely even to a pastime, be it polo or painting. War he "revelled in" because it made gigantic demands on the whole man.

Clearly, the whole Churchill was not going to be satisfied indefinitely with trench warfare. Indeed, he could not keep away from politics for long. He made a sudden sortie from the trenches in March, 1916, and, in his capacity of M.P., demanded a livelier conduct of the war. He stunned his listeners by proposing the recall of no less a deadhead than old Fisher as First Sea Lord. "We want Jacky!" shouted a crowd outside Parliament, drilled, it was thought, by Churchill himself. After this, even Violet agreed that her beloved Winston could suffer from strange aberrations.

In December, 1916, a violent shake-up in the political scene led Churchill to believe he would be restored to a prominent role in shaping war policy. Mounting dissatisfaction with the conduct of the war had prompted newspaper proprietor Lord Beaverbrook to conspire with Lloyd George to oust Asquith, and Bonar Law fell in with their plans. As Prime Minister of the new Coalition, Lloyd George wanted to include Churchill in his Government, but the Conservatives flatly refused. *The Times* learned of his exclusion with "relief and satisfaction." Churchill, said Gilbert, "felt humiliated and betrayed."

Only with difficulty did Lloyd George manage to install Churchill in the Cabinet (though not the inner War Cabinet) as Minister of Munitions in July, 1917. He was now a "Lloyd George man" in a coalition where the Conservative forces heartily detested him. For the remainder of the war, he did his work with ardour. Nevertheless, it is not for the manufacture of shells that Churchill is remembered. His fame has come to rest triumphantly on the telling of the story, rather than on the part he played in it. His *World Crisis* still reverberates with the thunder of terrible events. As a chronicle of the war, it will never be superseded.

There is space for only one brief example of his writing. Which shall it be? A heroic scene from the convoys plying the seas, or one of the last murderous thrusts by land, in both of which the United States played a crucial part? Or perhaps it should be Churchill's account of Armistice Day, 1918, half paean, half dirge. How on the "eleventh hour of the eleventh day of the eleventh month," all the links of discipline, brute force, self-sacrifice, terror, and honour, which had held the world together for four years, were broken—"every one had snapped upon a few strokes of the clock." That is a grim and gay unwinding. But in the end, it must be Churchill's picture of the Kaiser's Germany in its final convulsion. For this was in very truth the end of a chapter.

"The mighty framework of German Imperial Power, which a few days before had overshadowed the nations, shivered suddenly into a thousand individually disintegrating fragments. All her Allies whom she had so long sustained, fell down broken and ruined, begging separately for peace. The faithful armies were beaten at the front and demoralised from the rear. The proud, efficient Navy mutinied. Revolution exploded in the most disciplined and docile of States. The Supreme War Lord fled."

Falling Between Two Wars

*But now one can
see how lucky I was.
Over me beat the
invisible wings.*
CHURCHILL IN "THE GATHERING STORM"

FOX PHOTOS

As a "Lloyd George" Liberal, Winston Churchill found himself in a precarious position when the war ended. Like his leader, he had no secure political following. The party was split, "Asquithian" Liberals understandably loathing the faction which had destroyed them. Some of Lloyd George's personal unpopularity was bound to brush off on his colleagues. His discreditable traffic in the sale of honours, however, never for a moment contaminated Churchill. Like Wellington, Churchill shone and was seen to shine above the contemporary murk, untainted and incorruptible. But Churchill on his own account continued to attract special Conservative and Labour hostility.

To the Conservatives in the Coalition he was still a Liberal—at least in name—and not only a rat who had deserted their sinking ship in 1904, but now also a rat who continually poked his inquisitive and masterful nose into the niches they had acquired for themselves after clambering aboard the Coalition in 1915. Liberal Ministers had always been fairly good-humoured about the Churchillian habit of taking an interest in everybody else's business. Not so the Conservatives. Their leader, Bonar Law, was asked whether he would rather have Churchill for or against him. "Against, every time," he replied without hesitation, meaning that Churchill was impossible to work with.

Churchill's "uppishness" was largely due to an excess of energy and intellectual curiosity, rather than the conscious will to dominate. He was not an introspective person. The impression he made on others often escaped him. The British historian A. J. P. Taylor put it succinctly: "Churchill, despite his great qualities, lacked one gift essential to a statesman: he did not know how to put himself across." This was partly because he did not know himself. There was a paradox here; for he was a born actor, and putting himself across should have been his stock-in-trade. Lloyd George once wrote of him: "He is just like an actor. He likes the limelight and the approbation of the pit." He liked it, yes; but he would not or could not work for it consistently. It was only when the long inter-war period of 21 years was nearly over that he began to add to his brilliant repertoire of courage, vitality, and wit the ballast-virtues of patience and restraint.

Facing page: A double-decker bus burned in a London street during the General Strike of 1926.

71

POPPERFOTO

Churchill's transfer by Lloyd George to the Colonial Office in 1921 provoked several cartoons on his growing collection of "hats." Another satirist showed him trying on a "colonial" style hat with the comment: "Very becoming— but on the small side as usual."

If the Conservatives could not yet accept Churchill, the forces of Labour rejected him outright. Tension between them increased in 1919, when Churchill was upgraded from the Ministry of Munitions to that of Air and War. To be sure, some of his initial policies were conciliatory. He hastened the tormentingly slow demobilisation of the armed forces, and even tried to make those "hard-faced men who had done well out of the war" bear their fair share of post-war burdens by contributing to a Capital Levy.

Germany he wished to welcome into the newly formed League of Nations, although keeping her disarmed. He appreciated her legitimate grievances, later expressing his thoughts with memorable poignancy in *The Aftermath:* "Justice, that perpetual fugitive from the counsels of conquerors, had passed over to the opposite camp." When he came to write *The Gathering Storm,* the first volume of his history *The Second World War,* he denounced the vengeful and self-defeating Allied policy of squeezing Germany "till the pips squeaked" and making her pay "to the uttermost farthing." The "moral" he chose for the whole six-volume work has immense significance. It was a splendid pattern of a dozen words which he had earlier presented as the statesman's credo:

In War: Resolution
In Defeat: Defiance
In Victory: Magnanimity
In Peace: Good Will

Looking back on the years 1919–39, he could see that this moral had been ignored. Instead, the story of those 21 years seemed to have begun in mean-mindedness when magnanimity was needed, and ended in pliant good will when the time had come round again for resolution. The theme of *The Gathering Storm* he called:

How the English-speaking peoples
through their unwisdom,
carelessness, and good nature
allowed the wicked
to rearm

Meanwhile, Churchill's new duties in the War Office encouraged his natural bellicosity. When he assumed office in January, 1919, British and other Allied troops in Russia were caught up in the civil war between the Whites and Reds (Bolsheviks). The Bolsheviks had signed a separate peace with Germany in March, 1918, thus stranding in Russia large stores of Allied supplies. The Allies had sent in troops to protect these stores and to provide aid to the White Russians. With the Armistice in November, however, the Allies were undecided on which course to follow.

If the Cabinet and Allies wavered, Churchill did not. He abhorred the Bolsheviks; their atrocities appalled him. In *The Aftermath*, Churchill pinpointed Lenin as the embodiment of evil, equally terrible as friend or enemy: "His affections cold and wide as the Arctic ocean, his hatred tight as the hangman's noose." He wrote of Russia's sharpening her bayonets in her Arctic forests. Churchill pressed the Cabinet and the Allies to organise a war of intervention against Red Russia. His demands for armed intervention were rejected, but the lack of a decisive policy did allow

THE "BRITISH GAZETTE" AND ITS OBJECTS

Reply to Strike Makers' Plan to Paralyse Public Opinion

REAL MEANING OF THE STRIKE

Conflict Between Trade Union Leaders and Parliament

First issue of The British Gazette, *edited by Churchill. Accounts of violence were exaggerated, the main casualties being some burned-out buses.*

A few words are needed to explain the appearance of the " British Gazette."

There are at present two quite different disputes which are holding up the country. The first is the stoppage in the coal industry. This is a trade dispute which could be settled in the ordinary way. The Government have already paid a subsidy of twenty-three millions to give time for this industry to put its affairs on a sound basis. They cannnot, however, continue paying out between two and three millions a month of the taxpayers' money to the employers and workers in one particular trade.

Moreover, exporting coal at a loss to our rivals only increases their unfair competition with British manufactures. Lastly, if we go on subsidising our export coal Germany and other rivals will have to do the same. Thus every nation will be impoverishing itself in uneconomic competition. The coal industry must, therefore, come on to an economic basis.

The Coal Commission has shown how this can be done. The Government have accepted their proposals, and will carry out the recommendations affecting the State, even where this particular Government does not agree with them. But the owners and the miners must do their part as well. The owners have agreed to nearly everything recommended by the Commission; and it is certain that the small part to which they have not yet agreed would never be allowed to be the sole block to the scientific reorganisation of the Coal Industry.

policy, no better than drinking salt water to relieve thirst. No one has pointed this out more strongly than the wiser and more responsible Labour leaders.

If Parliament were to allow its considered judgment to be overborne under the cruel assault of a general strike, the economic disaster would only be a part of a much greater disaster. It would be definitely established that the weapon of a general strike which the Trade Union leaders at present wield is irresistible. These men, although it is certainly not the object of the great majority of them, would in fact become the masters of the whole country, and the power of government would have passed from Parliament into their hands. This would involve the virtual supersession of Parliament and of the representative institutions which we have established in our island after three hundred years of struggle, which we have preserved almost alone among the nations of Europe, and which are the foundation of our democratic freedom.

NO SECTIONAL DICTATION.

Instead of the representatives of the nation duly elected on a franchise almost universal, our rights and destinies would be in the hands of a body of men who, however well meaning most of them may be, represent only a section of the public and have derived no authority from the people comparable to that of the House of Commons. We must never forget, even in the heat and height of this struggle, that we are all fellow citizens. But the democratic State cannot possibly submit to sectional dictation. It is bound him to pour arms and supplies into Russia. After the last of the Allied forces were evacuated, Prime Minister Lloyd George announced the end of all forms of intervention.

Though the limited intervention had been carried out with Britain's Allies, Churchill's belligerent declarations made him the focus of Labour antagonism. The loyalties of the British Labour movement were to Socialism, and in no sense to Communism. But the war had reinjected them with a strong dose of pacifism. Moreover, the British war profiteers, deservedly caricatured in over-shiny top hats with heavy gold watch-chains across huge stomachs, appealed to them a good deal less than the Russian Reds.

In the early months of 1920, Churchill's attempts to help the Poles, who by now were battling the Russians, met with active Labour opposition. In May, dockworkers refused point-blank to load arms which they suspected were being sent to Poland. National demonstrations by the Labour party were followed by a vote in August to call a general strike should the Government continue giving aid to the Poles. The threat was enough; the Government capitulated.

That was the end of Churchill's interventionism. His defeat by the dockers gave organised Labour a sense of achievement and power which they never forgot. It also revived their angry, if to some extent apocryphal, memories of Tonypandy. But this time they had won.

Looking ahead for a moment, to 1926, Churchill was to get a bit of his own back, however unconsciously, during the General Strike. Since newspapers closed down during the strike, the Government put out *The British Gazette*, for which Churchill was given editorial responsibility. His zest for waging the class war during that week showed his love of a scrimmage. However, many people have felt that in becoming responsible for what was, in fact, a Government propaganda sheet, Churchill was temporarily prostituting those literary talents which had otherwise almost always worked on a grand and impartial scale.

Looking further ahead still, to 1942, Churchill and Stalin were to touch on Churchill's part in the war of intervention, during conversations in Moscow. "Have you forgiven me?" asked Churchill finally of a smiling Stalin. "Premier Stalin, he say," replied Interpreter Pavlov, "all that is in the past, and the past belongs to God."

In February, 1921, Churchill was named Secretary of State for the Colonies. In this office, he saw the need and opportunity to strengthen British imperial influence in the Near East and Ireland. "In Palestine," writes A. J. P. Taylor, "he was more nearly successful in reconciling Jews and Arabs than any other British statesman proved to be." His romantic imagination responded vividly to the inspiration of T. E. Lawrence. Churchill's daughter Sarah remembers Lawrence riding over to Chartwell on Sunday afternoons on his motorcycle and charming the children as well as their father. "Lawrence, despite all his profound dislike of publicity," said Winston, "had a remarkable way of backing into the limelight."

Ireland's corresponding hero was Michael Collins, whom Churchill came to admire for his romantic qualities as a guerrilla leader. The British government found itself forced to come to terms with "the gunmen," offering a treaty in 1921 which left the six northern counties under British control and made the rest of Ireland a self-governing Dominion as the Irish Free State.

Churchill's performance in Ireland was not noticeably superior to that of any other British statesman at the time. Before the volte-face of the 1921 Treaty, he had supported Lloyd George's coercion of Ireland through the disgraceful para-military police force called the Black and Tans. And the Treaty itself, signed by Ireland virtually under duress, led to the Irish Civil War of 1922 and incidentally to the death of Michael Collins.

As Colonial Secretary, Churchill also tried to play a dynamic political role in the highly inflammable affairs of Turkey and Greece. In the summer of 1922, the Turks were moving towards the Dardanelles in an effort to reconquer territory given to the Greeks at the close of the First World War. As the Turks approached the neutral territory occupied jointly by British, French, and Italian troops, the two latter forces withdrew, leaving only the British to hold the position.

The Cabinet decided the Turks must be stopped. Churchill's communiqué stating Britain's determination to meet force with force alarmed the British people, who wanted no more wars. It also infuriated the Foreign Secretary, George Curzon, who had not been consulted and complained bitterly of Churchill's interference. Though the Turks backed down, the incident caused the fall of the Coalition Government.

In the election of November, 1922, the Conservatives scored a sweeping victory. Churchill had stood as a Liberal in Dundee. As it happened, he had just gone down with acute appendicitis:

POPPERFOTO

Churchill as Chancellor of the Exchequer. The "hat" was undoubtedly larger, but the world of figures was always something of a "Wonderland" to him. Here he sets off to present his Budget with his parliamentary secretary, Robert Boothby, and his daughter Diana.

The General Strike of 1926. Baldwin's Conservative Government is looking for some way out other than a coal subsidy. Churchill sits at the table with Baldwin, Austen Chamberlain stands left, F. E. Smith smokes centre, and Neville Chamberlain stands on the ladder right.

THE MANSELL COLLECTION

"When I recovered consciousness," he wrote, "I learned that . . . I had lost not only my appendix but my office." Churchill was in the political wilderness and he did not enjoy it. "I like things to happen," a friend remembered his saying, "and if they don't happen I like to make them happen." But in the 1923 election, the only thing that happened to Churchill was another defeat, at West Leicester, where he stood as a Liberal Free Trader. What significant thing could he make happen except another change of party?

His fulminations against Bolshevism as "foul baboonery," and Socialism as "a serious national misfortune," were far more congenial to Conservatives than Liberals. "His tendency is all to the Right," wrote his friend Beaverbrook with satisfaction. The wheel was soon to come full circle. "I am a Liberal in all but name," he had written to his mother at 22. Now at 50 he could have said, "I am a Conservative in all but name." Indeed he had already dropped the name Liberal and was to describe himself between 1922 and 1924 as an Independent Constitutionalist—a singularly apposite title, as it happened, for his true political attitude throughout his life.

There were still two barriers between him and the Conservatives. Their policy of Protection was something Lord Randolph's son could not swallow. But when Stanley Baldwin, the new Prime Minister, got that bone out of the Conservative throat, Churchill had every reason for rejoining them—except a sense of decency. A man can rat but not re-rat, he himself had said. Churchill, however, had no alternative. With the decline of Liberalism and the rise of Socialism, there was no better hole to go to. Baldwin generously covered up any rodent traces by boldly appointing him Chancellor of the Exchequer. Churchill, with engaging humility, at first thought he was being offered the more lowly Chancellorship of the Duchy of Lancaster.

Suddenly Churchill, the wandering star, was again part of the great Conservative constellation. Asquith described him as an "Everest among the sandhills of the Baldwin Cabinet." Unfortunately, this five-year period, 1924–29, was one during which his political light burned dimly, or at least as dimly as it ever could in the Churchillian power house. The Exchequer did not suit his gifts. Financial riddles were not his forte. As a boy taking the Army entrance examination, he had described the mysteries of mathematics with whimsical amusement: "We were arrived in an 'Alice-in-Wonderland' world, at the portals of which stood 'A Quadratic Equation,'" followed by the "dim chambers" inhabited by the Differential Calculus and then a strange corridor of Sines, Cosines, and Tangents "in a highly square-rooted condition."

The Treasury remained something of a Wonderland to Churchill. But he took his officials' advice and put Britain back on the gold standard—not to her obvious advantage. If Churchill did not understand figures, he did appreciate gold. It suggested a return to the brave days of old when Victorian papas jingled golden sovereigns in their trouser pockets or, more elegantly, carried the delicious coins in a small sovereign-purse attached to the watch-chain. Being on the gold standard would enable the pound, he was assured, to "look the dollar in the face."

His officials would have been wiser to recall the words of a great orator from the land of the dollar: "You shall not press down upon the brow of labor this crown of thorns," declaimed William Jennings Bryan in 1896, inveighing against those who demanded that gold be the only monetary standard. "You shall not crucify mankind upon this cross of gold."

Notwithstanding the burden of the gold standard, the English-speaking peoples were to survive in prosperous complacency for a few more years, before the "Economic Blizzard" (Winston Churchill's name for the great depression) hit them in 1929.

———

Churchill had few close friends among politicians. Birkenhead, as has been said, was one of the few. Another who was to become a unique political adviser was Professor Frederick Lindemann (later Lord Cherwell), an Oxford scientist and sage. "The Prof," as he was universally known, had distinguished himself during the First World War by devising a theory of how to get a plane out of a spin and then testing his theory in person. Such a mixture of talent and courage could not fail to appeal to Churchill. Perhaps it was the Prof's esoteric taste in headgear which appealed to him at first. The Prof wore his famous bowler hat in all surroundings however rustic, from a shoot to a golf course. The thought of the brain inside the hat gave Churchill immense pleasure. "Prof, tell us in words of one syllable," said Winston at Chartwell, "and in no longer than five minutes, what is the Quantum Theory?" Winston timed the performance with his stopwatch, and at the end the whole Churchill family burst into spontaneous applause.

Max Beaverbrook's courage in fighting his asthma made as deep an impression on Churchill as the rest of his vibrant character. Close to him also were two young red-headed men: Duncan

POPPERFOTO

Right: Churchill swimming at Deauville. Below: Polo was still a favourite pastime. In this photograph, the strap on Churchill's right arm can be seen.

POPPERFOTO/CONWAY PICTURE LIBRARY

POPPERFOTO

Charlie Chaplin visited Chartwell in September, 1931. Churchill's daughter Sarah remembered him entertaining the family just before he left by seizing a stick and bowler from the cloakroom and doing his famous act. Left to right: Freddy (2nd Lord) Birkenhead, Winston, Clemmie, Diana, Randolph, Charlie Chaplin.

TERENCE LE GOUBIN/CAMERA PRESS LTD.

As he had after his downfall in 1915, Churchill turned to painting as a chief solace and pastime during his exclusion from the Government in the 1930s. He wrote: "Happy are the painters, for they shall not be lonely. Light and colour, peace and hope, will keep them company to the end, or almost to the end, of the day." This painting of Lady Castlerosse was one of his few portraits.

Sandys, who was to become Churchill's son-in-law by marrying Diana, and Brendan Bracken, who—according to a baseless legend—supposedly was Churchill's natural son. The legend amused Bracken enough for him to let it run without contradiction. For the rest, Churchill did not ordinarily depend on the handy small change of friendship. His genius was 90 percent self-generating.

His true friends were his ideas, and grandest of these was that of the British Empire. To him, it was the Empire alone which gave Britain her greatness. Britain without the Empire would be like Samson without his hair or Antaeus without his feet on Mother Earth. This Churchillian imperialism was to lead him again into the wilderness.

Conservative leader Stanley Baldwin and Winston Churchill were as different as the pipe from the cigar, which each respectively smoked. Though Churchill stoutly denied that a single rough word had ever passed between him and old "S. B.," they did not get on. Both were intense patriots. But whereas the Britain which Churchill loved was gallant and fierce, Baldwin's was little short of cosy; a pacific Britain, which would do anything for a quiet life. The final clash between them came over India.

The Labour party, under Ramsay MacDonald, had won the election of 1929 and Churchill was again out of office, though he remained part of the Opposition "Shadow Cabinet" headed by Baldwin. India's self-government had long been a plank of Labour; sometimes it was the key issue in their programme. Now they moved ahead, encouraged by the fact that Baldwin and the Conservative party supported the policy and by the friendship between the British Viceroy of India and Mahatma Gandhi.

India's well-respected leader, Gandhi, was a dedicated nationalist who preached the philosophy of *Satyagraha* ("truth-force"). From this positive philosophy issued, paradoxically, the double negative of non-violent non-cooperation with Britain. But it turned out to be a veritable double-headed axe against British imperial rule. The Viceroy was Lord Halifax, a Conservative and a future ambassador to the United States. He and Gandhi worked together for a peaceful solution to India's demand for freedom. Baldwin was sympathetic, Churchill outraged.

Even at his best, Gandhi appeared to Churchill no better than an astute politician who had enjoyed "commodious internment" in a British-Indian prison, only to win release and honour at the 1931 Round Table Conference in London. At their worst, Gandhi and his right-hand man, Jawaharlal Nehru, were seen by Churchill as "evil and malignant Brahmins" or even as wild beasts. "It is no use trying to satisfy a tiger by feeding it on cats' meat," said Churchill. As Gandhi did not eat meat of any sort, this metaphor lacked his usual felicity.

And yet Churchill's basic feelings towards India were not as "evil and malignant" (his words were to boomerang) as they sounded. A British historian, Robert Rhodes James, put the Churchillian attitude into correct perspective: "Winston Churchill's Imperialism was essentially nationalistic. The Empire was an instrument that gave to Britain a world position that she would not otherwise have had." Churchill was not a racialist tyrant. All he wanted was to make that "robust assertion of British Imperial greatness," for which Baldwin had neither the faith nor the stomach. Like Disraeli, Churchill saw India as the brightest jewel in Britain's crown.

Nevertheless, Churchill's deviation from his party's India policy did him present and future harm. It caused an irreparable breach with Baldwin and halted his renewed ascent in the Conservative party. In January, 1931, he sent into Baldwin his resignation from the Shadow Cabinet. Thus, like Sisyphus, he had painfully pushed his stone up the hill only to see it roll once more to the bottom.

In October, 1931, the great depression, which began with the Wall Street crash of 1929, finally dashed the Government to smithereens. When Labour was succeeded by the coalition National Government, Churchill hoped to help pick up the pieces. He was not invited to do so. His account of the rebuff is a beguiling example of wry and rueful humour: "Like many others, I had felt the need of a national concentration. But I was neither surprised nor unhappy when I was left out of it. Indeed, I remained painting at Cannes while the political crisis lasted. What I should have done if I had been asked to join I cannot tell. It is superfluous to discuss doubtful temptations that have never existed."

Churchill was working on his monumental *Life of Marlborough* and planning his *History of the English-Speaking Peoples*. It was not his fault if he had to paint or write while Rome burned. If he had had his way, he might have been fiddling also. At 11 he had asked his parents to let him learn the cello, but received the usual no for an answer. He ended his reflections on his 1931 ostracism philosophically: "Political dramas are very exciting at the time to those engaged in the clatter and whirlpool of politics, but I can truthfully affirm that I never felt resentment, still less pain, at being so decisively discarded in a moment of national stress."

He was indeed far away from the "clatter and whirlpool;" beached, like one of the boats he painted. He had lost his friend Birkenhead through an untimely death in 1930, and Lloyd George was out of the arena, recovering from an operation. Had Churchill's star set? Not at all.

"There was much mocking in the Press about my exclusion," he remarked of a similar situation four years later. "But now one can see how lucky I was. Over me beat the invisible wings."

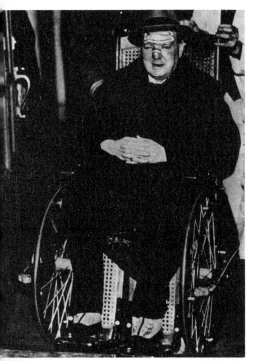

Churchill after his accident in New York at the end of 1931. He got out of his car on the wrong side and was knocked down by a taxi. When recovered, he invited the driver to come round and celebrate.

POPPERFOTO

The austerities which the National Government imposed on all but the rich were later described by Churchill as "an earlier version of 'blood, sweat, toil, and tears,'" but without the stimulus of "war and mortal peril." War was in fact not so far off, and that other stimulating presence, Churchill himself, was already alerted. But whereas in the early forties he was to speak with the voice of Macaulay's Horatius ("Now who will stand on either hand, And keep the bridge with me?"), in the late thirties his was the disregarded voice of Cassandra.

The great depression, which raged across the world from Wall Street to the Reichsbank and on to the City of London, had struck Germany with splintering force. Inflation had ruined the middle classes; unemployment now ruined the workers. There was a man ready and waiting to make the German Republic's difficulty his own opportunity.

Adolf Hitler had given up his reputed career as a house painter some 18 years before Churchill was landscape painting at Cannes. Hitler's failed Munich *putsch* of November, 1923, had landed him in gaol. While Churchill was composing his *World Crisis*, Hitler was writing *Mein Kampf*. He came out of prison in December, 1924, a few weeks after Churchill had re-entered the British Cabinet. Hitler's nine months of imprisonment, wrote William L. Shirer, "far from discouraging him, had charged him with a new, fanatical faith in his destiny." Churchill's faith in his destiny was just as strong, but at present more nebulous. Ten years later, when Hitler had become Fuehrer, Churchill's destiny was becoming clearer, though in a sense he was still waiting in the wings.

Churchill's one dramatic event between the end of 1930 and mid-1935 was a visit to the United States for a lecture tour and narrow escape from death in a traffic accident. "On December 13

[1931] when on my way to visit Mr. Bernard Baruch, I got out of my car on the wrong side and walked across Fifth Avenue without bearing in mind the opposite rule of the road which prevails in America, or the red lights, then unused in Britain. There was a shattering collision. For two months I was a wreck." Then he "crawled back" to health, spent 40 nights giving lectures and 40 days on his back, and for the rest of 1932 "lay pretty low."

Between building water-gardens for goldfish and walls and a cottage at Chartwell, and dictating articles—all "very pleasant" occupations—he was launching his great parliamentary speeches against the Nazi menace. On March 14, 1933, for instance, he rebuked the Air Ministry: "I regretted to hear the Under-Secretary say that we were only the fifth air power . . . . I was sorry to hear him boast that the Air Ministry had not laid down a single new unit this year. All these ideas are being increasingly stultified by the march of events. . . ." Directing events that marched or even galloped had always been Churchill's metier. After the Government of India Bill became law in 1935, despite the efforts of his India Defence League, he could train his guns on Hitler alone. This meant a concentration of fire and, more important, in time an accumulation of allies.

Towards the end of 1935, there was another general election. Baldwin, having won a huge overall majority, again saw no reason to include Churchill in his Cabinet (though he later wisely put

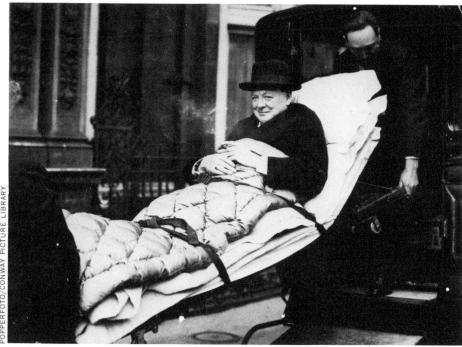

Going home after a bout with paratyphoid in 1932.

POPPERFOTO/CONWAY PICTURE LIBRARY

POPPERFOTO

POPPERFOTO

Left: Churchill's union card as a bricklayer, issued in 1928. Right: Building at his home, Chartwell, in 1930. He completed the garden walls, the waterworks for his goldfish, and a cottage before the outbreak of the Second World War.

him on the Air Defence Research Committee). Off went Churchill once more to sunnier climes, this time to Barcelona, Tangier, and Marrakech, with his paint box. Meanwhile a bombshell exploded at home. The Foreign Secretary's attempt to appease Mussolini at the expense of Abyssinia (the Hoare-Laval Pact) was indignantly repudiated, Sir Samuel Hoare resigned, and Anthony Eden became Foreign Secretary.

"Better stay away," warned Churchill's friends. To return now, during this crisis, would only seem a personal challenge to the Government. So he stayed on painting until near the end of January, 1936, when King George V died and King Edward VIII ascended the throne.

The new young King was more concerned about the unemployed than about Hitler. He and the Government attached little importance to the League of Nations as an instrument for collective security against aggression. Hitler, from his angle, attached even less. On March 7, 1936, he invaded the Rhineland. To Churchill, this meant war was inevitable.

He longed to assist in preparing his country's defences. But Baldwin, who had been considering a Cabinet reshuffle, felt less inclined that ever to annoy Hitler by including the bellicose Churchill. Thus was Churchill preserved yet again from becoming involved in the political equivocations of the next three years. He wrote: "This is not the first time—or indeed the last—that I have received a blessing in what was at the time a very effective disguise."

The blessing returned in even heavier disguise, so to speak, at the end of the year.

By the beginning of December, Churchill had succeeded in organising a left-right-and-centre movement against Hitler called "Arms and the Covenant." On December 3, a meeting was held in the vast Albert Hall at which Churchill and Trades Union officials spoke—together at last. On the same day the Abdication crisis broke.

For many months, a counterpoint to the crescendo of martial music had been audible to those with ears to hear. The new melody was a love song. King Edward had become passionately attached to Wallis Warfield Simpson, but unfortunately this intelligent and charming young American from Baltimore had been married twice already, and both her previous husbands were living. Popular feeling in Britain and the Commonwealth, for which Baldwin proved to be the catalyst, quickly crystallised against the idea that their King should make a morganatic marriage. The King abdicated on December 11, 1936, and was succeeded by his brother, King George VI. The crisis proved to be a nine-days' wonder. But those nine days were long enough to send Churchill yet again, in the manner of Sisyphus and his stone, to the bottom of the hill.

With typical romantic impulsiveness, Churchill had proclaimed his unconditional allegiance to King Edward on the very first day, at the Albert Hall meeting itself: "We are going to sing 'God Save the King,'" he announced from the platform. "I shall sing it with more heartfelt fervour than I have ever sung it in my life."

His fervour never ebbed. In Parliament, he was shouted down when he tried to put the King's case. "Sit down! Shut up! Twister!" Even when the King himself had settled for abdication, Churchill was still entreating him to hold on and give his supporters time to rally. Churchill's exhortations to the King remind us of his words to the South African engine driver in 1899—"Buck up a bit. I will stick to you"—and foreshadow those to the British nation in 1940. He was a man of courage who had been born to fortify others—though on this occasion, he later admitted, he had backed the wrong cause.

His was the most moving comment on Edward VIII's abdication. Thumping out the rhythm with his stick on the gravel drive of Fort Belvedere, the King's country retreat until he abdicated, Churchill recited the verses which Andrew Marvell had written three centuries before on the execution of King Charles I:

He nothing common did or mean,
Upon that memorable scene.

Then Churchill himself resigned his own future to oblivion: "All the forces I had gathered together on 'Arms and the Covenant' . . . were estranged or dissolved, and I was myself so smitten in public opinion, that it was the almost universal view that my political life was at last ended."

POPPERFOTO

A royal romance.
Above, King Edward VIII
and Mrs. Wallis Warfield
Simpson on the Dalmatian
Coast, August, 1936.
Right, the ex-King and
his bride.

POPPERFOTO

Yet the truth was that Churchill's star was preserving him from the taint of yielding to temptation. How strong could be the temptation to appease Hitler was demonstrated most tragically by the Munich Agreement of 1938.

Just to ignore Hitler was a temptation. Churchill's beloved United States had not been able to resist it, and he rebuked the Americans gently in *The Gathering Storm:* "Absorbed in their own affairs and all the abounding interests, activities, and accidents of a free community, they simply gaped at the vast changes which were taking place in Europe, and imagined they were no concern of theirs."

Even Churchill had had his early moments of illusion, when Hitler seemed a possible leader for Germany and Mussolini not at all a bad fellow. However, in the last critical three years before the war, though Churchill's final break with the Establishment over the Abdication relegated him to the role of a voice crying in the wilderness, the voice cried loud and clear. He said of the Government in 1937, for instance, that they were "decided only to be undecided, resolved to be irresolute, adamant for drift . . . all-powerful to be impotent." As each sinister event brought Europe a step nearer to the abyss, Churchill at least was there to present the issues sharply, unfudged by hopes or fears. The rearming of Germany; Anthony Eden's courageous resignation from the Foreign Office over the appeasement of the Axis powers; the rape of Austria and Czechoslovakia; Hitler's final coup in signing the German-Soviet pact—all these events, as well as his visit to the Rhine front in August, 1939, were the subject of Churchill's valuable memoranda on Britain's preparedness.

Munich was a turning point in Churchill's political career, although no one appears to have realised it at the time. Prime Minister Neville Chamberlain flew back from Germany delighted. Hitler, it seemed, had been thoroughly appeased by the cession of the predominantly German areas of Czechoslovakia: now, it also seemed, he had no more territorial demands to make in Europe—it would be "peace for our time." Amid the intense euphoria of relief, Churchill struck an unequivocally discordant note in the House of Commons: Munich was "a total and unmitigated defeat." Privately he declared, "The Government had to choose between war and shame. They chose shame, and they will get war too."

It was not long before Churchill was proved right. In March, 1939, German tanks were rumbling into Prague; Czechoslovakia ceased to exist as an independent state.

POPPERFOTO

Chamberlain returns from Germany, claiming to have brought "peace for our time." Churchill denounced the Munich concessions as "a total and unmitigated defeat."

Thus Churchill acquired the moral force of having been right —no longer the voice in the wilderness, but more and more thunderously a voice echoed by popular sentiment. Few could deny that he had the spirit and determination to stand up to dictators. In peace, certainly unpredictable and eccentric. But now a growing number of his countrymen felt that he was desperately needed in the Government; that Britain in her extremity needed such a daring pilot.

In this period only his painting suffered. "I found painting hard work in this uncertainty." But his brick-laying flourished. There was something reassuring about brickwork. Its lines had to be straight, regular, and orderly, qualities which Churchill liked in all of life's endeavours. If the Government could not think straight and in an orderly fashion, at least Churchill's children should be taught to do so. "Thank you, my darling, thank you," he would say to a child who had succeeded in making a point. "You have put it very clearly."

His overalls and trowel were equally reassuring, since they meant that the cottage he was building would be ready to receive Clementine and Diana and Randolph and Sarah and Mary when war came. He had been laying bricks at this cottage for a year. Now, in September, 1939, the last room—the kitchen—was finished.

POPPERFOTO

As the Second World War drew nearer, public opinion demanded the return of Churchill to the Government. In this Punch *cartoon of July, 1939, he is seen as Drake before the arrival of the Spanish Armada.*

His Finest Hour

Never give in. Never give in.
Never, never, never, never, never—in nothing
great or small, large or petty—never give in
except to convictions of honour and good sense.
CHURCHILL AT HARROW, 1941

POPPERFOTO

As the Second World War opened, Churchill's mood was solemn and historical, with just the requisite dash of drama. The drama was shown by his resolve to take personal precautions against possible Nazi assassins. He pressed Inspector W. H. Thompson, a retired Scotland Yard detective, back into service as a bodyguard, and they slept and watched alternately, both of them armed. Like many others in England at that time, including the editor of a highbrow literary magazine, Churchill was proud to rate himself Hitler's Public Enemy No. 1.

The solemnity of the hour overwhelmed him in the House of Commons. He had just listened to the first air-raid warning. Though there were no bombs as yet, the sirens alone were enough to kindle Churchill's imagination: "I felt a serenity of mind and was conscious of a kind of uplifted detachment from human and personal affairs. The glory of Old England . . . filled my being and seemed to lift our fate to those spheres far removed from earthly facts and physical sensations."

On that same day, September 3, 1939, Prime Minister Chamberlain had offered Churchill a seat in the War Cabinet as First Lord of the Admiralty. This was history repeating itself with a vengeance, or rather, with a pardon. For Churchill was once more sitting in the chair at the Admiralty from which he had been ignominiously expelled in 1915. Behind him was the identical map of the North Sea on which he had charted the movements of the German High Seas Fleet.

How tempting for him to see the war of 1939–45 as a repeat performance of 1914–18. But historical analogies could be deceptive. In a sense, the British Grand Fleet had changed more than the First Lord of the Admiralty. It was vulnerable now to air attack. Similarly, Churchill's friend Bracken believed that the Army had changed more than the future Minister of Defence. "Bear in mind," he was to say when the same Churchill who had helped develop the tank failed to grasp its full capability, "that Winston always remains the 4th Hussar."

But if history occasionally fitted her devotee with blinkers, the effect of his historical antennae was far more often enlarging

Facing page:
"London can take it."
Fires rage around
St. Paul's Cathedral
during the London
Blitz.

Churchill arriving at the Admiralty on September 4, 1939. Prime Minister Chamberlain had invited him to join the War Cabinet as First Lord of the Admiralty, the post he had held at the beginning of the First World War.

POPPERFOTO

and liberating. On September 2, the day before Churchill became First Lord again, the House had listened to a "temporising" statement from Chamberlain about the crisis. It was received with fierce impatience. Arthur Greenwood then rose to speak for the Labour Opposition. "Speak for England," cried Leo Amery from the Conservative benches. Chamberlain winced. But Churchill could have thought of no more glorious task for himself. To speak for England—Old England, all England, his England—this was "living History," as he had said to Margot Asquith a quarter of a century ago. History was to live again. But after a strange nine-month gestation.

THE WAR THAT WASN'T

"Willing to wound, and yet afraid to strike." Alexander Pope's line seemed to sum up the mood of both sides, once Poland had been overrun and partitioned between Hitler and Stalin. "The Twilight War" or "The Trance" were romantic titles chosen by Churchill to describe this period of inactivity on the Western battlefield. Others preferred the more vivid transatlantic term, "Phony War." Nevertheless, "twilight" was an apt enough description. That autumn and winter must have reminded Churchill of the long empty months before the Battle of Jutland. Churchill's ships were again waiting in the perpetual twilight of the northern seas. In his eyes, the present duties assigned to the Admiralty offered equally dim prospects. "Convoy and Blockade," as he called it, was no doubt an essential service. But it was not his idea of waging naval warfare against Germany. Nor was it the public's. His pride was hurt when people asked "What is the Navy doing?" Were there no alternative lights in the gloom? He had his own aggressive answer: "First and foremost gleamed the Baltic."

The Baltic, it will be remembered, had featured in Churchill's dreams for 1915. They were never realised. Now he planned to attack Germany through the hard underbelly of her iron ore supplies, located in Sweden, but shipped during the winter months

A Cabinet group in November, 1939. Churchill is standing second from the left, Lord Halifax is seated on the extreme left, and Chamberlain is seated in the centre.

POPPERFOTO

KEYSTONE

Churchill in France as First Lord of the Admiralty, January, 1940, with (l-r) General William Ironside, General Alphonse Georges, General Maurice Gamelin, and Lord Gort.

from the Norwegian port of Narvik. If the Navy could deny the port, and thus the iron ore, to German trade, this might be more than a mere Baltic gleam; it could be the dawn.

Soviet Russia's attack on Finland, which began on November 30, 1939, furnished Churchill with added reasons for operations in this area. Though these incentives disappeared when, after a magnificent resistance, Finland made peace under duress in March, 1940, Churchill's strategy had meanwhile expanded.

The Allies believed that Hitler was preparing to violate Scandinavian neutrality. Hitler, who in fact had no such immediate intention, at the same time became aware of Allied proposals to make a pre-emptive strike. The whole thing was redolent of the past. In 1807, the British had got wind of a plot by Napoleon to seize the Danish fleet. They acted accordingly, capturing the Danish fleet themselves. The only difference in 1940 was that it was to be the German dictator who made the successful pre-emptive strike.

The sequence of events made curious reading afterwards.

The heroic episode of H.M.S. *Cossack* and the *Altmark* set the ball rolling on February 16. A German vessel, the *Altmark*, loaded with British prisoners of war, was chased by destroyers

F. Kersting

Blenheim Palace where Churchill was born.
The palace was a gift of the British people
to his ancestor John Churchill,
first Duke of Marlborough.

Churchill attends a luncheon given by new Lord Mayor
of London, Sir F. Newson Smith, at Mansion House.

Popperfoto

Imperial War Museum

Churchill and Roosevelt meet at the Citadel, Quebec,
for the First Quebec Conference on August 18, 1943.
In the front row are Roosevelt and the Earl of Athlone,
Governor-General of Canada. Standing are Canada's
Prime Minister, Mackenzie King, and Churchill.

Keystone Press

Churchill, Roosevelt, and Stalin at Yalta in February, 1945. Here plans were completed for Germany's defeat and occupation. Roosevelt died two months later.

Churchill visits General Montgomery's 21st Army Group Headquarters at the Normandy beachhead shortly after the landing in June, 1944. At left is Field Marshal Sir Alan Brooke. In the background are the 21st Army's Headquarters trailers.

Imperial War Museum

Fox Photos

Sir Winston inspecting troops at Dover Castle
after his installation as Lord Warden of the Cinque Ports.

Churchill, Eisenhower, and Premier Joseph Laniel of
France at the Big Three Conference in Bermuda.

Keystone Press

Winston Churchill becomes
"Sir" Winston when he is invested
with the Most Noble Order of the
Garter at Windsor, June, 1954.

Fox Photos

Chartwell, Churchill's home in Kent where he spent nearly forty years. "... A day from Chartwell is a day wasted...."

A. F. Kersting

Churchill's studio at Chartwell with his paintings on display.

Keystone Press

Churchill's funeral, St. Paul's Cathedral, London.

Fox Photos

Keystone Press

Portrait by Sir Winston of his father, Lord Randolph Churchill.

The famous Karsh photograph of Sir Winst

Churchill's funeral, St. Paul's Cathedral, London.

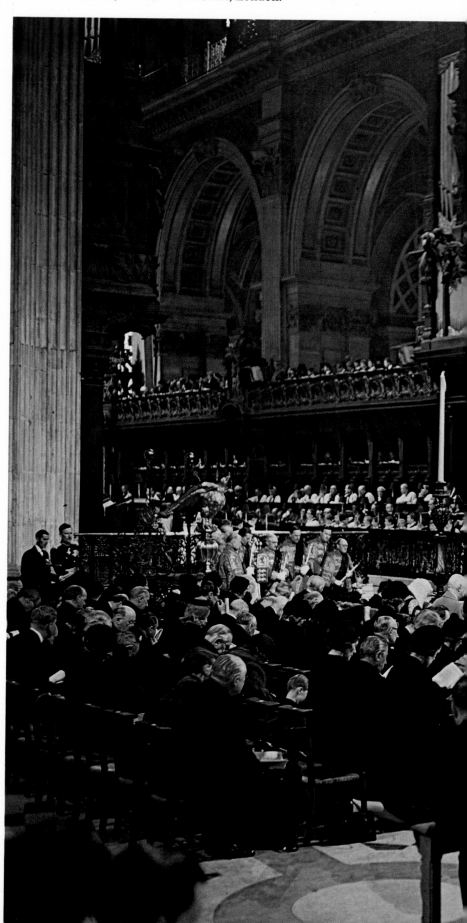

Fox Photos

Aerial view of Bladon Church near Blenheim,
where Sir Winston was buried on January 30, 1965,
after the state service at St. Paul's Cathedral. He
chose to lie beside his father, mother, and
brother in this country churchyard.

Syndication International

IMPERIAL WAR MUSEUM

_The First Lord of
the Admiralty discusses
plans with Lord Gort,
Commander-in-Chief of
the B.E.F., during his
flying visit to British
General Headquarters
in France._

and took refuge in a Norwegian fiord. Churchill personally
ordered H.M.S. *Cossack* to board the *Altmark* and free the prisoners. It turned out that 299 captives were battened down below
decks in storerooms and even in an empty oil tank. And the
Altmark, despite her assurances, was not unarmed. "The Navy
is here!" was now the cry, instead of that unhappy murmur, "What
is the Navy doing?" Unfortunately, however, Hitler also noted
the cry and drew his own conclusions. "The Navy is here" could
only mean that it was there by Norwegian invitation. From
February 16 onwards, Hitler planned that the German forces
should go in.

On April 4, Chamberlain delivered an encouraging address
to the Conservative party. One thing was certain about Hitler,
he declared: "He missed the bus."

On April 8, "Operation Wilfred" began. The British Navy laid
mines in Norwegian waters, preliminary to making landings at
Narvik, Trondheim, Bergen, and Stavanger. Ironically, the mine-
laying operation distracted the Norwegians from the activities of
their real enemy.

And on April 9, in the twilight before dawn, Hitler's forces
invaded Norway and Denmark. "Operation Wilfred" had been

narrowly beaten by what must surely be called in retrospect "Operation Bus." For the bus which Hitler was thought to have missed had in fact been boarded by him and his staff and, with Hitler at the wheel, was knocking down Chamberlain and the British Cabinet like ninepins.

Even Churchill's devoted admirer, General Sir Ian Jacob of the War Cabinet Office, admitted that the Norway campaign showed Churchill's weaknesses. The Admiralty's acting in isolation, as if this were still the First World War, was one weakness. Liddell Hart added another: the extension of the war into Scandinavia. For unless Hitler's reinforcements could have been cut off—which they could not—the Germans were "bound to gain a growing advantage."

Churchill's strengths were no less obvious. There were "occasional flashes of brilliance," said Jacob, as in the destroyers' successful action at Narvik. What struck Jacob even more was Churchill's personal energy. Much better informed and more eager than any of his colleagues, Churchill was "in hourly contact with events."

The Norway campaign ended in disaster. Naval losses were heavy: the aircraft carrier *Glorious,* two cruisers, nine destroyers. "Failure at Trondheim! Stalemate at Narvik!" This was Churchill's gloomy summary of the operations up to the first week in May, 1940, when most of the Allied expeditionary forces withdrew. In June, Norway surrendered, and the British evacuated Narvik. Considering Churchill's own prominent part in the fiasco, it was a marvel that Parliament did not totally reject him, as it had after Gallipoli. Again, however, there were differences between past and present. For one thing, he had been right about Hitler between the wars when most of the rest were wrong. He had therefore accumulated a large capital sum of national respect. For another, the parliamentary storm was to break over the Prime Minister, rather than over the First Lord of the Admiralty. In 1915, it had been otherwise. Above all, the fate of the Prime Minister and the Norwegian campaign was to be overshadowed almost at once as the Phony War came to a dramatic end. And so, looking back, Churchill ended his account of the Scandinavian misadventure with his usual optimism: "We thought fortune had been cruelly against us. We can now see that we were well out of it."

POPPERFOTO

Churchill behaved with pugnacious loyalty throughout the parliamentary turmoil which erupted on May 7, 1940. The same voice —that of Leo Amery—which had cried to Labour on September 2, 1939, "Speak for England," now cried to Chamberlain: "You have sat too long here for any good you have been doing. Depart, I say, and let us have done with you. In the name of God, go!" Amery was quoting the lethal words hurled at the Long Parliament by Oliver Cromwell. Far from echoing them, Churchill described them as "terrible words coming from a friend."

The next day, Lloyd George plunged in his knife. If Chamberlain called for sacrifice, let him lead the way; let him "sacrifice the seals of office." The First Lord of the Admiralty, added Lloyd George, should not allow himself to be made into an "air-raid shelter" for his colleagues.

Shades of Gallipoli. But in those days the term was "scapegoat," not "air-raid shelter."

Nevertheless, the First Lord was more than willing to let his stricken leader take any shelter he might find in the Churchillian oratory. Churchill wound up the debate in a hubbub of Opposition jeers, aimed not at him but at Chamberlain. When the vote was taken, some 100 Conservatives either abstained or supported the Opposition. Passions rose. Chamberlain left the House to a chant of "Go, go, go, go!" and a Labour member singing *Rule Britannia*.

British troops during the disastrous Norwegian campaign.

115

Churchill still urged his leader to stick it out. But Chamberlain was keyed to sacrifice and foresaw a Government of all parties.

In that event, Churchill could foresee himself at the helm, especially after a meeting on May 9 with Labour leaders Clement Attlee and Arthur Greenwood at No. 10 Downing Street. They considered it unlikely that Labour would serve under Chamberlain. Churchill maintained a calm, both internal and external, which he had learned during his years in the wilderness. "The prospect neither excited nor alarmed me. . . . I was content to let events unfold." In this uncharacteristically passive mood he sat in the sunlit garden of No. 10 with Lord Halifax, talking, as he said, about "nothing in particular." But Churchill must have been listening for the beating of what he called "the invisible wings." For these two were in fact the candidates for Chamberlain's post.

THE BATTLE OF FRANCE

On the fateful morning of May 10, it was tanks which the world heard, not wings. Hitler's blitzkrieg had begun. Without warning, Belgium and Holland had been invaded before dawn.

A drama was meanwhile being enacted in Downing Street, a drama as quiet and circumscribed as the assault on the Low Countries was deafening and widespread. At 11:00 a.m. Churchill, Chamberlain, and Halifax met to discuss the selection of the nation's leader at this most crucial of all hours. For a moment the diviner's rod quivered over Halifax. Chamberlain preferred him. The Palace preferred him. (King George VI's father had labelled Churchill "impossible" during the First World War.) Many Labour leaders preferred him because of his progressive policy in India. But Halifax could not prefer himself. He believed that a wartime leader must be in the House of Commons. In any case he had little appetite for the role.

Churchill, meanwhile, had taken no part in the discussion. "Usually I talk a great deal," he recalled, "but on this occasion I was silent." Violet Asquith remembered him being silent only when he was painting. This must have been another moment of silence, a golden one. He listened to Chamberlain's preliminary weighting of the scales against him. Then followed a very long pause, longer, it seemed to Churchill, than the Two Minutes' Silence on Armistice Day. At last Halifax broke it, to make his renunciation. "By the time he had finished it was clear," wrote Churchill, "that the duty would fall upon me—had in fact fallen upon me." Then Churchill spoke, expressing readiness to form a

116

Government of all parties as soon as he had received the King's commission. Suddenly the tension snapped, and conversation returned to normal.

The scene had been tremendous, and all played their parts with credit. One small query, however, remains. Churchill's silence was so out of character, risking as it did the loss of his life's ambition, that a doubt arises in regard to the curtain-raiser in the garden with Lord Halifax. Even if they said "nothing in particular" to one another, faces can speak as well as lips. Churchill must have scanned Halifax's features anxiously and seen there the expression of a man who did not aspire next day to shoulder the supreme burden of state.

Churchill's audience with King George VI brought him pleasantly down to earth. After a searching and critical look, the King said, "I suppose you don't know why I have sent for you." "Sir, I simply couldn't imagine why." The King laughed and relaxed. "I want to ask you to form a Government."

The King and Chamberlain may have had their doubts about Churchill. But Churchill walked on air, or, as he put it, "with Destiny." He has recorded his feelings on going to bed at 3:00 a.m., Prime Minister at last. "I felt as if I were walking with Destiny, and that all my past life had been but a preparation for this hour and for this trial." Many and many a time, he had had the sensation of being preserved for something. On May 10, 1940, he knew what it was. That old feeling had not been a classic case of "infantile omnipotence," as some psychiatrists might suggest. Rather, it was the ever-hopeful reaction of a genius hitherto manqué. Now the genius was to flower in its natural habitat, head in the sunshine and roots in the scorched earth of war.

Only one reason was advanced by Churchill for his sense of "profound relief" at becoming Prime Minister. "At last I had the authority," he wrote, "to give directions over the whole scene." To his countrymen, however, the profoundest relief was in hearing a voice which could "speak for England."

The author can remember the thrill of his first broadcast. It was a thrill half of horror at the ferocity involved in war-making, half of excitement at the sudden appearance of a leader with the will to win. "My policy is to wage war," said the minatory but measured voice. "War without stint: war to the uttermost."

Churchill, who had also assumed the post of Minister of Defence, repeated his theme to Parliament on May 13 in a magnificent speech: "I have nothing to offer but blood, toil, tears, and sweat.... You ask, What is our policy? I will say: It is to wage war, by sea, land, and air, with all our might and with all the strength that God can give to us: to wage war against a monstrous tyranny, never surpassed in the dark, lamentable catalogue of human crime."

Lewis Douglas has pointed out the remarkable resemblance between Churchill's stirring words and those of the French Premier, Georges Clemenceau, when France was *in extremis* in 1917. Clemenceau said: "In domestic policies I wage war; in foreign policies I wage war; always everywhere I wage war.... before Paris I wage war; in Paris I wage war; behind Paris I wage war.... I wage war until the last quarter hour because the last quarter hour will be ours."

"The Tiger" was Clemenceau's nickname. Churchill had actually seen and heard the Tiger on that critical day in 1917, pacing to and fro, "growling and glaring" like a wild animal. Now in 1940, he himself conveyed a feeling of that same growl and glare to his parliamentary audience. With his keen ear for oratory, his sense of history, and his wonderful memory, Churchill would naturally have found the great French orator coming to his aid in his hour of need. As Douglas said, Clemenceau had been called in to save France, Churchill to save Britain; each proved to be a saviour of the Western World.

On May 13, the very day that Churchill was offering blood, toil, tears, and sweat to Britain, the Germans broke into France at Sedan. They too, it seemed, had a sardonic sense of history; for Sedan was the scene of France's disastrous defeat by Germany in 1870. And when France was defeated again 70 years later, Hitler was to dictate his armistice terms in the same railway carriage in the forest of Compiègne as the French had used to present their terms to Germany in 1918. Hitler danced a jig.

In Britain, people listened, appalled, on their wireless sets to the fall of France, enacted blow by blow five or six times a day. The German advance soon became a broad panzer-tide which none could hold. Churchill flew out to Paris on May 16, after being awakened the day before by Premier Paul Reynaud's voice on his bedside telephone: "We are beaten; we have lost the battle.... We are defeated; we have lost the battle." In Paris, Churchill asked General Maurice Gamelin, "Where is the strategic reserve?" Gamelin shook his head, shrugged his shoulders, and replied, "*Aucune.*" There was no need to translate.

POPPERFOTO

Churchill at
No. 10 Downing Street,
May, 1940. Harold
Nicolson, the M.P. and
diarist, described
Churchill's eyes after he
became Prime Minister as
"glaucous, vigilant,
angry, combative,
visionary and
tragic."

POPPERFOTO

Or as Churchill
said, "In defeat, defiance."

On May 20, Gamelin was replaced by General Maxime Weygand as Commander-in-Chief. It could make no difference, since both of them, and even Churchill himself, were still thinking in terms of 1918, as Churchill afterwards confessed. He tried to encourage his French allies by reciting his own experience of the German 1918 offensive, which came to a halt for lack of supplies and was followed by an Allied counterattack. "I learned all this," said Churchill, "from the lips of Marshal Foch himself." Alas, the lips of Foch—he had commanded the Allied forces in 1918—had spoken without knowledge of the tanks of Hitler. According to Liddell Hart, Churchill's misapprehension of the blitzkrieg led him to urge upon the Allies a 1918-type of "furious, unrelenting" counter-offensive which, if it could have been mounted, would have been overrun, destroying their last chance to escape the panzers.

Their last chance was in fact to stand on their river lines, or "water lines," as Churchill called them. By May 24, however, that hope too was spent. The British and French armies were straining and struggling towards a totally different "water line"—the Channel. General Heinz Guderian's panzer corps had reached the sea near Abbeville. Boulogne and Calais were next to fall. The Allied armies in Belgium were thus cut off. On his own initiative, the British General Lord Gort began his march to the sea, where a single harbour still remained open near the Franco-Belgian frontier—Dunkirk.

Meanwhile, the ordeal endured in France had its repercussions on Churchill. Guderian's rampaging panzers had taught the French one key fact about modern warfare: the indispensability of air cover. The French desperately needed fighter planes to tackle the German dive-bombers. Anguished appeals poured in from the French for ten more British fighter squadrons . . . ten more . . . ten more. The agony was almost as great for Churchill. He was torn between the moral responsibility to help an ally and the overriding duty to protect his own country.

For weeks on end, the unavoidable but searing conflict raged between the two loyalties. Sir Ian Jacob and Air Chief Marshal Dowding have each vividly described some of the scenes at No. 10 Downing Street, where the War Cabinet sat with their advisers. There were dramatic clashes on May 15. Ten more squadrons of Hurricanes had been demanded by the retreating French. At the Chiefs of Staff meeting in the morning, it was decided that no more should be sent. But that afternoon, the argument broke out again in the sunlit garden of No. 10. This informal discussion caused Churchill to have second thoughts. The next morning, the decision of the 15th was reversed. Four squadrons were to be sent after all. It was the only occasion when Jacob remembered Churchill changing his mind once he had made it up.

Churchill himself described the sequel to the meetings of May 15 and 16. On the 16th, he had flown to Paris and seen first-hand the desperation of the French. Churchill wired back to England, urging a further gesture to their ally, and obtained the sanction of the War Cabinet for sending six more squadrons to operate over France, though from British bases. "Ten fighter squadrons! . . . In this way I hoped to revive the spirits of our French friends, as much as our limited means allowed." In the small hours of May 17, a poignant scene was enacted in Paul Reynaud's flat, when he and Edouard Daladier, the French Foreign Minister, received the tonic news. "Daladier never spoke a word," wrote Churchill. "He rose slowly from his chair and wrung my hand." The indomitable Churchill got back to bed at the British Embassy about 2:00 a.m., to sleep well despite air raids and cannon fire. He had been Prime Minister for seven days. After May 19, when the last of the promised Hurricanes had been despatched, there were to be no more.

But the fighting in France was to continue for another terrible fortnight, and French appeals for Churchill to send Hurricanes did not cease. A final tug-of-war was recalled by Dowding. He argued vehemently at No. 10 for sending *none*. Suddenly, he rose to his feet with a graph of losses in his hand, walked around the table to the Prime Minister, and laid the graph before him with the words, "If the present wastage continues for another fortnight we shall not have a single Hurricane left in France *or in this country*." He pronounced the last four words with ominous emphasis. No one spoke. Churchill continued "glaring down at the graph." Though still hideously torn, he realised that Dowding's case was unanswerable.

In his *Mémoires,* General Weygand was to ask a bitter question. Was it "absurd" to think that the Royal Air Force, which later reduced German aviation to impotence during the Battle of Britain, could have inflicted considerable losses on those same German bombers during the Battle of France? General Weygand's son, Jacques Weygand, reprinted the tortured question in the biography of his father, though only in a footnote.

We now know that the two situations were in no way comparable. Fighter Command won the Battle of Britain because it

"At last I had the authority," Churchill wrote upon becoming Prime Minister, "to give directions over the whole scene." The energetic Churchill took an intense interest in all aspects of the war effort. Here he inspects coastal defences on the northeast coast of England.

POPPERFOTO

Inspecting the 15th Scottish Division. This face and posture gave him heart.

JOHN COLVILLE, CB, CVO

IMPERIAL WAR MUSEUM

Churchill watches troops demonstrate a battle course.

Carrying his gas mask, Churchill inspects the House of Commons Home Guard.

THE MANSELL COLLECTION

operated from highly organised airbases with radar and sophisticated control systems. Operating from improvised airbases in France, they could not long have survived. Nor did the Royal Air Force gain such an easy ascendancy over German aviation as Weygand suggested. The Battle of Britain was to be "a near run thing."

To return to Dunkirk. Personal intervention by Hitler was soon to affect Britain's fortunes. The escape from Dunkirk, popularly known as a "miracle" but more accurately described by Churchill as a "deliverance," took place between May 26 and June 4. Without disparaging for one moment the British and Allied heroism which made that deliverance possible, the historian must point out that Hitler himself, ironically, was one of the deliverers. We know from captured German documents that Hitler temporarily halted Guderian's tanks just when they were all set to reach Dunkirk first. If Hitler had not interfered, could the Dunkirk deliverance have occurred? And why did he interfere? No one can now read Hitler's mind. But one probable explanation is that Hitler was reserving the panzers for the advance over the Somme and leaving the Luftwaffe to deal with the British Expeditionary Force.

That said, the glory and glow of the Dunkirk deliverance will not fade. The figures alone tell a heroic tale: 338,226 British, French, and Belgian troops brought back to England when only some 45,000 had been hoped for; and over 200 gallant craft sunk by German bombs during the operation out of the 860 involved. Churchill makes special reference to what he calls "the great tide of small vessels [which] began to flow towards the sea, first to our Channel ports, and thence to the beaches of Dunkirk and the beloved Army."

Like all superb enterprises, Dunkirk had its griefs. One was almost literally a postscript. The 2,000 courageous Frenchmen who had acted as the rearguard could not be saved. They were among those taken prisoner. This increased French soreness over the fighter squadrons.

Churchill himself had two outstanding Dunkirk "moments." The first was early on, when he outlined the grim prospect to Parliament. "The House should prepare itself," he warned on May 28, "for hard and heavy tidings." Everyone knew his words meant the possible extinction of the B.E.F. Then he filled in the lurid details at a special meeting for 25 Ministers of Cabinet rank outside the War Cabinet. When he reached the words, "Of course, whatever happens at Dunkirk, we shall fight on," all 25 Ministers burst into cheers, some even running round the table to thump the Prime Minister on the back. He wrote afterwards, "There was a white glow, overpowering, sublime, which ran through our Island from end to end."

Lord Halifax, a sincere Christian and conscientious "appeaser" of Hitler, according to the categories of those days, was not present. (As Foreign Secretary, he was a member of the War Cabinet.) We now know that on May 28, the very day of the ministerial demonstration, Halifax had argued with Churchill on behalf of his group for a negotiated peace. That Churchill never mentioned this fact in the course of his whole six-volume history *The Second World War*, though not surprising in a man of his strong loyalties, is nonetheless admirable. As Dr. Patrick Cosgrave, the British writer, asked of those who accuse Churchill of suppressing facts unfavourable to himself, what about May 28, 1940, when he suppressed facts favourable to himself and unfavourable to the appeasers?

The second great moment for Churchill occurred on June 4, when "Operation Dynamo" (the Dunkirk evacuation) was officially declared complete. His speech on that day to Parliament was described by Harold Nicolson, M.P., in a letter to his wife as "the most magnificent" he had ever heard. There were many pregnant and salutary passages in the body of the speech, like "Wars are not won by evacuations." But it was the tremendous peroration which echoed round the world: "Even though large tracts of Europe and many old and famous States have fallen or may fall into the grip of the Gestapo and all the odious apparatus of Nazi rule, we shall not flag or fail. We shall go on to the end, we shall fight in France, we shall fight in the seas and oceans, we shall fight with growing confidence and growing strength in the air, we shall defend our Island whatever the cost may be, we shall fight on the beaches, we shall fight on the landing-grounds, we shall fight in the fields and in the streets, we shall fight in the hills; we shall never surrender. . . ."

Equally acceptable to the defiant Commons was Churchill's unique pronunciation of the words "Gestapo" and "Nazi." He managed to inject 100 percent of "growl and glare" into his snarling vowels. The Americans, of course, could not *hear* his splendid growls. But the end of the speech was read in the United States with marked appreciation: "And even if," concluded Churchill, "which I do not for a moment believe, this Island or a large part of it were subjugated and starving, then our Empire beyond the seas, armed and guarded by the British Fleet, would carry on the struggle, until, in God's good time, the New World, with all its power and might, steps forth to the rescue and the liberation of the Old."

As he sat down and the cheering broke out, he was heard by those next to him to murmur: "We'll beat the b——s over the head with broomsticks; it's all we've got."

Though Churchillian references to "our Empire" might not appeal in America, the overall tone and wording of his peroration were miracles of dignity and tact. Until after Pearl Harbor, Churchill's relations with the New World were bound to be delicate. Better than any other man, Churchill knew that in the long run Europe's survival depended on American military intervention. Yet he could never quite say so in terms. All he could do was somehow bring the magic words "New World" or "United States" into all his greatest speeches.

One important question remains in regard to Churchill and Dunkirk. How essential were his own unwavering courage, buoyancy, and even bounce, in sustaining the spirits of his hard-pressed countrymen?

Churchill himself insisted until the end of his life that the whole English-speaking world was cast in a heroic mould; all he needed to do was give expression to their resolve. "It was the nation and the race dwelling all round the globe that had the lion's

Cheers for Churchill from the 15th Scottish Division.

JOHN COLVILLE, CB, CVO

heart. I had the luck to be called upon to give the roar." At least one British historian, Liddell Hart, finds himself in substantial agreement with Churchill's modest self-assessment. Liddell Hart wrote: "The British have always been less dependent than other people upon inspiring leadership. . . . It may be a necessity when they are weary, but not when they have had a slap in the face. It was Dunkirk that braced them in June 1940, more than any individual influence."

Nevertheless, a vast weight of independent testimony, not to mention personal experience, brings this author down on the other side. Churchill was indispensable. In the words of the American Professor Marder, who made a close study of Churchill's role at the Admiralty: "Churchill had a unique capacity to inspire others well beyond the limits of what they supposed to be their own capacity." Or in the answer of Britain's Sir Isaiah Berlin to his own question: did Churchill *create* or merely *reflect* the spirit of "No-surrender" in 1940? "He created a heroic mood," replied Berlin, where the prevailing mood was "stout-hearted but unorganised," in fact "confused." After Churchill had roared, the confusions sorted themselves out into a grand imperturbability. And Churchill "had a lion's share in creating it." Even after Churchill had been roaring away for a whole year, the editor of *The Times*, Robin Barrington Ward, noted in his diary that it was good to see Churchill's "cheerful, challenging—not to say truculent look."

June, 1940, was a terrible month for Churchill and a tragic one for France. On June 5, in what has become known as the Battle of France, the Germans crossed the Somme and attacked along a 100-mile front. The situation had reached Tiger Clemenceau's final stage—"behind Paris I wage war"—when Churchill flew out for the fourth time. He met Paul Reynaud near Orleans on the 11th, shortly before the French Government moved to Tours. The conflict between defence of "the Island," as Churchill called Britain, and support for her Allies became ever more acute. Looking back on it, Churchill wondered how, with France evidently falling, "we had the nerve to strip ourselves of the remaining effective military formations." These were the 52nd Lowland and 1st Canadian Divisions. Churchill told Reynaud that whether France "in her agony" capitulated or not, the British would "fight on for ever and ever and ever." To Weygand, who asked what the British would do if 100 German divisions landed on their soil, Churchill replied, "*Nous les frapperons sur la tête*"—We would hit them on the head as they crawled ashore. It was an echo of Wellington's famous answer to the question what *he* would do if well and truly cornered by the enemy. "Give them the biggest thrashing of their lives."

The next morning, before returning to England, Churchill took the French Admiral Darlan aside. "Darlan, you must never let them get the French fleet," he said solemnly. Darlan promised.

His fifth visit to France was made on June 13. He was not to return for four years. His most vivid memory of his few hours in Tours was General Charles de Gaulle standing "stolid and expressionless." Churchill murmured (in French) for De Gaulle's ears alone: "The man of destiny." On June 14, the Germans entered Paris.

By June 16, half of the French Cabinet was pressing for an armistice, with the other half in favour of carrying on the war from North Africa. To prevent French capitulation, Churchill proposed to Reynaud the formation of an Anglo-French Union—the imaginative plan of Monsieur Monnet, Lord Halifax, and others, not at first considered practicable by Churchill. Despite Reynaud's efforts, the French Government, now at Bordeaux and dominated by the defeatist Marshal Henri Pétain, had utterly rejected the Union with Britain. It would relegate France, so they said, to the status of a British Dominion. In any case, in three weeks' time "England will have her neck wrung like a chicken," and union with her would be "fusion with a corpse."

Late that night, the 16th, Pétain formed his "Armistice Government" of surrender to Hitler. Next evening, Churchill broadcast a generous epitaph on France as Britain's ally, ending with the words, "the genius of France will rise again." And that same evening, General Edward Spears flew in from Bordeaux to Britain. With him was General de Gaulle, and in Churchill's words, "De Gaulle carried with him, in this small aeroplane, the honour of France."

On June 18, Churchill spoke to Parliament. He announced the fact that Britain now stood alone, and against yet another enemy, for Italy had declared war against the Allies on June 10. "What General Weygand called the Battle of France is over. I expect that the Battle of Britain is about to begin. Upon this battle depends the survival of Christian civilisation. . . . Hitler knows that he will have to break us in this Island or lose the war. If we can stand up to him, all Europe may be free and the life of the world may move forward into broad, sunlit uplands. But if we fail, then the whole world, including the United States . . . will sink into the abyss of a new Dark Age, made more sinister, and perhaps more protracted, by the lights of perverted science. Let us therefore brace ourselves to our duties, and so bear ourselves that, if the British Empire and its Commonwealth last for a thousand years, men will still say: 'This was their finest hour.' "

Churchill happened to be speaking on the 125th anniversary of Waterloo Day. Britons had long been accustomed to think of June 18, 1815, as their finest hour. But now a new grandeur had been added. At Waterloo, Britain had not stood alone.

Churchill was able to draw comfort even from what was now to prove the crowning horror of the French tragedy. The German armistice terms had convinced him that Darlan's fine French fleet would pass fully armed into German control. On July 2, he therefore gave Darlan the choice of joining the British Navy, sailing to a British port or to the French West Indies, or sinking his fleet within six hours. The French replied that their warships would never fall intact into German hands—but any British attempt to intervene would be met with force.

Force did indeed meet force on July 3, and "Operation Catapult" resulted in the destruction of an important part of the French fleet at Oran. It was sunk by the British.

Today a school of thought holds strongly that the tragedy of Oran was avoidable. But for Churchill's impulsiveness—his "within six hours"—the British and French admirals on the spot could have negotiated terms. Churchill himself, however, quoted the "immense relief" of America at the sinkings. "The Atlantic Ocean seemed to regain its sheltering power," he wrote. World opinion was both shocked and impressed. "It was made plain," said Churchill, "that the British Government feared nothing and would stop at nothing."

A brief month separated the Battle of France and the Battle of Britain. During that lull, many people must have wondered what sort of man this new Prime Minister really was. Perhaps the best way to describe the man is through the eyes of some of his colleagues, whose memoirs of their years with him have been compiled by Sir John Wheeler-Bennett in *Action This Day: Working with Churchill.*

The contributors, writing independently, had all served at various times on Churchill's staff. Two of them, General Sir Ian

Jacob and Edward Bridges (later Lord Bridges), produced an intriguingly similar account of Churchill's first impact as Prime Minister. Bridges, Secretary to the Cabinet, wrote: "It was as though the machine had overnight acquired one or two new gears . . . ." Jacob, the military man, already knew something of Churchill's reputation for brilliance marred by unpredictability, meddlesomeness, verbosity, and abrasiveness. He and his colleagues frankly dreaded Churchill's arrival. Afterwards Jacob admitted their mistake. "We had not the experience or the imagination to realise the difference between a human dynamo when humming on the periphery and when driving at the centre." Dunkirk had been named "Operation Dynamo." Now the dynamo was in Downing Street.

Drive was universally recognised as one of Churchill's major gifts. It was symbolised in many engaging ways. He sent a Christmas greeting to his Secretariat: "A busy Christmas and a frantic New Year." He also used scarlet labels bearing the words "Action This Day" which he stuck at the top of urgent letters. Not everyone liked these red-hot sparks from the Prime Minister's furnace. But they kept the staff on their toes. Did Churchill copy the idea from that vehement influence in his earlier life, Admiral Fisher? If Fisher saw anyone standing idle, as he thought, at the Admiralty, he would stick onto him a scarlet label with the word "RUSH."

But even a dynamo has to be harnessed to a machine. This was the aspect of Churchill's functions which he found least agreeable and his staff most onerous. He was no orthodox administrator. He concentrated on the essentials and ignored the rest. Towards the end of the war, "the rest" would lie unregarded in his boxes of staff memoranda, telegrams, and correspondence, to be marked R ("Return") or RWE ("Return at Weekend").

Not that he was allergic to detail. Far from it. Like an industrious bee, his mind flew from detail to detail when the blitz began. He dipped into the question of heating in air-raid shelters and probed the problem of bombs on the Zoo. After seeing a blitzed restaurant in Margate with the proprietor's family in tears, he took up the question of compensation for war damage. But the details had to be of his own choosing.

This brings us to the place of "self" in Churchill's universe. He has sometimes been called positively selfish. This is misleading. Those who worked with him admitted that he was self-centred. He was not a conversationalist but a monologuist. His set-pieces were nevertheless so brilliant that few listeners wished to inter-

IMPERIAL WAR MUSEUM

rupt. Similarly, they recognised that he was self-centred precisely because he had an interior vision which must be brought into the light of day. They felt privileged to assist.

Nor did he give the faintest hint of that frigidity, meanness, and intolerance which often keep the egoist going along his narrow path. Churchill was a free ranger. If he followed his hunch rather than his agenda, that was the way of genius.

It is sometimes asked whether he did not browbeat his staff. We are offered the portrait of a tyrant riding roughshod over his experts and only taking the advice of his personal friends, if them.

It is true that Churchill's Chiefs of Staff had to put up with much rough usage. That they were willing, even proud, to do so was a tribute both to them and him. He liked interminable discussions. This was partly for the pleasure of argument; he had been a pugnacious Parliamentarian for some 45 years and particularly enjoyed the free-for-all of Question Time in the House of Commons. But chiefly he went on arguing because he realised that as long as he kept an argument going it could not be won by his opponents. If in the end he was worsted, he would put the matter, as he said, "on the hob." This meant leaving it to simmer until he

The Prime Minister at work while travelling by train.

131

JOHN COLVILLE, CB, CVO

Above: Churchill in a Cromwell tank. His Service friends agreed that he never quite grasped the full capability of tanks. Below: With a young friend in Cairo, 1942. "All babies look like me," Churchill once said.

IMPERIAL WAR MUSEUM

had found fresh fuel to bring it to the boil again, and to win. Very exhausting no doubt for his staff. And his daily—and nightly—routine did nothing to ameliorate their lot.

He woke at 8:00 a.m., rang for his breakfast and boxes, and applied himself to both of them in bed. Then he got up, worked with his staff, had his first meeting at 11:30 a.m., and lunched. In the afternoon, he slept for at least an hour, undressed in bed if possible, and if not, in his car with his eyes covered. There were more meetings from 6:00 until dinner at 8:00, followed perhaps by a film-show or an occasional game of bézique or Corinthian bagatelle. At 10:00 or 10:30 p.m., the final meetings of the "day" began. They nearly always went on until 2:30 or 3:00 a.m. Churchill at 65 could function perfectly on six and a half to seven hours sleep, especially as he slept like a baby as well as looking like one. ("All babies look like me," he once said.) His staff had to share his long hours but could not indulge in his afternoon siestas.

Sometimes he would snap at them. "The Prime Minister wishes it to be recorded," minuted J. R. ("Jock") Colville, a private secretary at No. 10, "that the expression 'most grateful' is not to appear in any letter for his signature. He says that he is the only person who can decide whether he is most grateful or not."

Sometimes he would shout at them: "Who was the fool who did this?" For a lion, it seems, must roar even at his friends. But though he acted the ogre, he did not mean his act to be taken too seriously. He explained to Sir John Martin, another private secretary at No. 10: "I may *seem* to be very fierce; but I am fierce only with one man—Hitler." Jock Colville said: "He pretended to a ruthlessness which was entirely foreign to his nature."

It was the same with animals and children. He was tender-hearted. Once he had said good morning to it, no animal on his Chartwell farm was allowed to be killed for food. Nor was corporal punishment ever administered to his family. When Churchill's *My Early Life* was published in 1930, the present author was somewhat startled by his view that schoolboys should be "whipped hard" for writing bad English. It was a relief to learn from his daughter Sarah's *A Thread in Tapestry* that the small Churchills could be as bad as bad and still not be smacked but only banished from the presence.

IMPERIAL WAR MUSEUM

Churchill with Admiral Sir John Tovet (right) and Sir Stafford Cripps. An austere Labour leader who joined Churchill's Cabinet, Cripps said: "I never minded being called by Winston Churchill late at night, or even in the early hours of the morning, for it was then that you really got down into his mind."

In fact, both Churchill's staff and children remember him as one who never bore a grudge—"anyway not for very long," said Sarah—and who created a warm family circle from which none was excluded. He gave his staff complete confidence, treating them as members of the family at Downing Street and even more so at Chequers, the Prime Minister's official country house in Buckinghamshire. Churchill liked to call them his "Secret Circle," not because the circle was in any sense official, much less an underground society, but because the name emphasised his trust in them and was fun. His military staff saw everything, and his secretarial staff everything except the dates of military operations and the special "yellow boxes" containing enemy documents.

If there were staff and ministerial criticism over many of Churchill's methods and heart-burning over some of his decisions, these did not have to be hidden. No official ever lost his job because he differed from Churchill.

His impatience was proverbial. His judgment of men was uncertain, though it did not lack brilliance, as in the appointment of Lord Louis Mountbatten (later Earl Mountbatten of Burma), first as Chief of Combined Operations and then to Southeast Asia Command.

Nor did his wartime premiership suffer from quarrels between the Service chiefs or between them and the civilian Ministers. This had been the bane of Asquith's Cabinets in the First World War. Lord Alanbrooke, formerly General Sir Alan Brooke, Chief of the Imperial General Staff, later said: "The P.M. [Prime Minister] prevented any quarrelling between the three Services and co-ordinated their work."

Moreover, Churchill's conversation and speech-making, inside and outside No. 10 Downing Street, besides being irradiated by his unique eloquence and wit, included jokes against himself. During a bad stretch of the war he was to say of the Churchill tank: "As might be expected it had many defects and teething troubles, and when these became apparent the tank was appropriately christened 'The Churchill.' " His eloquence and epigrams were always used in the cause of action, as in June, 1941, when he said, "The only answer to defeat is victory."

Towards the end of the war, he was much put out by the changes in spelling and pronunciation of foreign place names being adopted by the Foreign Office and the B.B.C.—Ankara for Angora, Istanbul for Constantinople. Churchill concluded a magnificent tirade to the Foreign Office: "Foreign names were made for Englishmen, not Englishmen for foreign names."

This, then, was the man who, from Downing Street and from Chequers, from his bed and from his desk, from Parliament and from the places where people gathered to listen to the radio, was to lead Britain into battle.

THE BATTLE OF BRITAIN

"We have got into the final, and it is on the home ground." Those words might well have been Churchill's introduction to the Battle of Britain. In fact, they were the remark of some humble, anonymous citizen. But they expressed everyone's feelings. Better to look at Hitler's promised invasion as a sporting event rather than as Armageddon.

The "sporting event" was known to the German High Command as "Operation Sea Lion." It had its own problems. By July 31, Admiral Erich Raeder had convinced Hitler that no invasion of Britain could be attempted until Hermann Goering's Luftwaffe had driven the Royal Air Force out of the skies. "Operation Sea Lion" was accordingly postponed until mid-September, 1940. Meanwhile, Goering set the crucial date for "Eagle Day." That was the day on which the Luftwaffe would commence its intensive air war to knock out the R.A.F. After this, the fleet of barges already assembled in the captured ports of France and Belgium would carry the invaders to Britain.

Pitted against the waves of bombers escorted by Messerschmitts would be a British Fighter Command substantially stronger than the world suspected. In May, 1940, Churchill had appointed his friend Max Beaverbrook to head up the new Ministry of Aircraft Production. By mid-July, the aircraft workers had replaced all the 400 planes lost over France. At the end of the year, Britain had over 4,000 fighters; Germany's production figure for the year was only just over 3,000. Dowding called the results achieved by Max "magical."

Dowding's headache was the shortage of skilled pilots. The Germans had as many skilled pilots as they could use. And 400 of their best, shot down by the R.A.F. and held prisoner in France, had been handed back to the Luftwaffe by the Vichy government, an act which Churchill could never quite forget or forgive. There were 1,434 British and Allied fighter pilots at the beginning of August; combat losses brought the total down to 840 at the beginning of September. Could these few save Fighter Command's airfields, and so Britain?

POPPERFOTO

RADIO TIMES HULTON PICTURE LIBRARY

*Bomb damage,
Buckingham Palace.
Queen Elizabeth said:
"Now I can look the East
End in the face."*

*December, 1940.
Churchill toured the
London docks after a
heavy German raid. On
Mrs. Churchill's left is
Brendan Bracken.*

POPPERFOTO

The parliamentary debating chamber was destroyed on the night of May 10, 1941, the first anniversary of Churchill's war premiership.

Below, left: Churchill boards the Naval auxiliary patrol vessel in which he travelled to visit London's docks. Below, right: With Clemmie on the River Thames. Churchill is wearing his famous "John Bull" hat.

IMPERIAL WAR MUSEUM

IMPERIAL WAR MUSEUM

"Eagle Day," August 13, dawned in thick cloud unfavourable to the Luftwaffe. (It happened to be Blenheim Day also, the day on which Marlborough won his great victory, surely a good omen for Churchill.) Nevertheless, the Luftwaffe flew 1,485 sorties. The clouds did not clear till the 15th; but even then, despite a supreme effort of 1,786 German sorties, the skies were not cleared of the R.A.F. The German eagle of "Eagle Day" went on flying and dropping his bombs until the 18th. By now the eagle was a slightly bedraggled bird. And his friend the sea lion had not even got his flippers wet. There was a lull for a few days.

The morale of the Messerschmitt pilots had not been raised by Goering's constant accusations of failure. The morale of the pilots flying Spitfires and Hurricanes, armed with their eight Browning guns apiece, was sublimely uplifted by Churchill's speech of August 20 to the House of Commons: "Never in the field of human conflict was so much owed by so many to so few."

On August 24, the battle for the skies began again. But at the end of this second bid by Goering, the scales were manifestly tipping to Britain. On September 7, a new phase began, the bombing of London. Once more the invasion barges were at the ready.

That afternoon, an air armada 1,000 strong bombed London's East End and docks, followed the same night by further mass attacks. This was the beginning of the London Blitz. Five days

IMPERIAL WAR MUSEUM

While touring London's dock area, Churchill saw two workmen having their dinner. He asked, "Are you managing to get plenty of food?" They replied, "Aye sir! We are doing grand, thank you."

IMPERIAL WAR MUSEUM

January, 1941.
Churchill speaks to
dockyard workers on a
ship he visited.

later, the pilot of a Stuka unerringly but misguidedly dive-bombed
Buckingham Palace. The King and Queen had a narrow escape.
So even the Royal Family were in it. Queen Elizabeth said: "Now
I can look the East End in the face." The people in their homes
and factories, in the shelters and in the Underground, on the roofs
doing plane-spotting, beneath the streets disposing of time-bombs,
manning the anti-aircraft batteries and balloon barrage, all said:
"London can take it." In Churchill's words, they were "grim
and gay."

The Local Defence Volunteers, created earlier to resist and
capture German parachutists, and rechristened by Churchill the
Home Guard, had been training madly and joyously. They positively longed for action. The ringing of church bells was to signify
a German landing. The author and her few-weeks-old baby were
awakened one night that September by unmistakable chimes. So
this was it. But why did nothing more happen? It was a false
alarm. The Home Guard had interpreted the ultimate code word,
"Cromwell," indicating "invasion imminent," to mean "readiness
for immediate action." In future, the Home Guard had to *see* at
least 25 German parachutists before ringing the bells. Churchill
good-humouredly called the chaotic events of that night "a useful
tonic and rehearsal."

He visited the ruins of workshops and homes, looking alternately like a glum and savage tiger and a cheerful cherub. The
we-can-take-it spirit produced his famous V-for-victory sign.
When he toured the blitzed houses with the King and Queen,

Churchill visits a village during an exercise by Home Guards. Local school children were among the "invaders," and a small boy caused great amusement by aiming a toy revolver at the Prime Minister from behind a farm cart barricade.

IMPERIAL WAR MUSEUM

he wore a conventional suit and his much admired high-crowned round hat; when on his own, he would sometimes sport his beloved boiler suit. He knew that Goering's attacks on London had in fact saved the terribly strained and depleted Fighter Command. London's ordeal—57 nights of bombing—was a "saving factor" in the country's defence.

In October, Hitler formally postponed the invasion till 1941. His thoughts were already turning eastwards. A month later, on November 14, Goering changed his tactics to the night bombing of British cities, starting with Coventry. No more than London did Coventry, Birmingham, Southampton, Liverpool, Glasgow, Bristol, or any of the others, flinch. There was a horrific incendiary bombing raid on London on December 29. Churchill called it "an incendiary classic."

The Blitz ended on May 16, 1941. "Sea Lion," thoroughly flea-bitten and discredited, was postponed again, meeting his "demise," as Churchill put it, on September 15, 1942. The Luftwaffe had gone East—to Russia.

Churchill's concluding words for the year 1940 echoed the spirit of the Abbé Sieyès when asked what he had done during the French Revolution: *"J'ai vecu"*—"I survived." Churchill wrote: "We were alive." Then he proceeded to count his blessings, beginning with national freedom. "There had been no invasion of

140

the Island." Moreover, he said, referring to the British rout of the Italian armies, "Victory sparkled in the Libyan desert." This would not have been possible but for Churchill's heroic step of August, 1940, in sending half of his best available tanks to Egypt, despite the invasion menace at home. (Unfortunately, early in 1941, a sense of obligation and perhaps a harking back to Gallipoli 1915 were to cause Churchill to transfer men and materiel from North Africa to Greece, where he not only failed but allowed Germany's General Erwin Rommel to reoccupy Libya.)

To return to Churchill's blessings. Most heartening of all, "across the Atlantic the Great Republic drew ever nearer to her duty and our aid."

This is the moment to review briefly the actual aid which America, since the war began, had sent to a sinking Europe and its off-shore island. American aid had helped to keep that island afloat.

Exactly a week after Britain declared war on Hitler, President Franklin D. Roosevelt was writing the first of his wartime letters to Churchill—the first of 800. Churchill was to contribute over 900. Reminding Churchill that they had occupied similar posts in the First World War—Roosevelt had been Assistant Secretary of the Navy—the President generously invited Churchill to keep him personally in touch "with anything you want me to know about." Churchill responded "with alacrity" (his words). He had hitherto set eyes on Roosevelt only once in his life, when Roosevelt visited Britain "in all his youth and strength." Since then, Roosevelt—at the age of 39—had been stricken with polio. When the Second World War broke out, he had five and a half more years to live, while Churchill, though eight years older than Roosevelt, had a quarter of a century. Roosevelt moved around in a wheelchair. But it was a chair which enthroned him in millions of hearts, both for his personal courage and his lively sympathy with the sufferings of others. His New Deal in social welfare had raised America from the cruel disillusionment of the great depression.

Throughout the Phony War the two corresponded, Churchill while at the Admiralty always signing himself "Naval Person." When he became Prime Minister, he changed his signature to "Former Naval Person," but the naval bonhomie between them increased.

The first fruits of this association had appeared in November, 1939, when the United States Neutrality Act was repealed. Britain

JOHN COLVILLE, CB, CVO

A pensive Churchill in his high-crowned round hat.

141

benefited from the new principle of "Cash and Carry." For though in theory all belligerent powers now had the right to carry American munitions in their ships, in practice Britain still ruled the waves. On May 15, 1940, that black day of Reynaud's heart-cry, "We have lost," the Prime Minister had written to the President asking for the loan of 40 or 50 over-age U.S. destroyers and also aircraft, anti-aircraft equipment, ammunition, and steel. Three days later, the President had signified his eagerness to facilitate the Allied governments' obtaining everything in Churchill's second category. (During June, 43 million dollars' worth of surplus stock was sent.) The destroyers, however, would mean an approach to Congress, for which "the moment was not opportune." Congress still had its powerful isolationist bloc, and F.D.R.'s close friend Samuel Rosenman remembered the President once saying to him: "It's a terrible thing to look over your shoulder when you are trying to lead—and to find no one there."

With the "carry" question solved, Britain's "cash" problems multiplied. All too soon her dollars would be exhausted. What then? Roosevelt had an answer: "I am trying to eliminate the dollar mark." By September, 1940, he was able to give Britain the 50 destroyers in exchange for a 99-year lease of air and naval bases in the West Indies and elsewhere. This was to be expanded into what Churchill called "the glorious conception" of Lend-Lease.

The next step was personal contact. In January, 1941, the President sent his closest confidante, Harry L. Hopkins, to Britain to assess the situation. He was probably Churchill's most important visitor of the whole war. Hopkins was to perform all his miracles for Britain as a chronically sick man. "There he sat," wrote Churchill, "slim, frail, ill, but absolutely glowing with refined comprehension of the Cause." He was like "a crumbling lighthouse" whose beam nevertheless "led great fleets to harbour." This was not merely metaphor. The Battle of the Atlantic against German submarines had still to be fought and won.

That the first over-age destroyers were far from being a "great fleet" did not escape Churchill's notice. "Cheap and nasty," he is said to have muttered under his breath. When Hopkins looked startled, Churchill added aloud: "Cheap for us and nasty for the enemy."

Churchill, nevertheless, was profoundly grateful. Hopkins sent back to Roosevelt a message as penetrating as it was persuasive: "Churchill is the government in every sense of the word—he controls the grand strategy and often the details—labor trusts him—the army, navy, air force are behind him to a man. The politicians and

IMPERIAL WAR MUSEUM

Harry L. Hopkins
accompanied Churchill and his
wife on a tour of Glasgow,
January, 1941. As liaison between
Roosevelt and Churchill,
Hopkins was Britain's most
important visitor of the war.
Churchill paid tribute to
his "refined comprehension
of the Cause."

upper crust pretend to like him. I cannot emphasize too strongly that he is the one and only person over here with whom you need to have a full meeting of minds." To Churchill himself, Hopkins quoted the words from the Book of Ruth: "Thy people shall be my people and thy God my God—Even to the end." Churchill's eyes filled with tears.

The Lend-Lease Act was passed by Congress in March, 1941, "the most unsordid act in the history of any nation," as Churchill said. In time to come, he was to pay a characteristic tribute to the superb effectiveness of Hopkins. If Hopkins ever became a peer, he would have to take the title of Lord Root of the Matter.

THE BEAR BAITED

In a sense it was the Axis powers, Germany and Japan, who went to the root of the matter in 1941. The year was one of startling paradox. Two hideous catastrophies turned out to be cases of Churchill's famous "blessings in disguise," at least for the Island. The first was Hitler's invasion of Russia in June; the second, the Japanese bombing of Pearl Harbor in December. The "Russian bear," as Churchill liked to call the Soviet Union, had given Napoleon a death-hug in 1812 from which he never recovered. The bear was to do the same to Hitler. Russia's size and Russia's winters had not changed. It was to Churchill's great credit that he, the communist-hater *par excellence,* immediately welcomed the bear as an ally.

A few days before the news of Hitler's expected attack on Russia arrived, Churchill was strolling on the lawn at Chequers, discussing with his secretary, Jock Colville, the prospects of an Anglo-Russian alliance. Surely, suggested Colville, this would place him, the arch anti-communist, in an awkward predicament. Churchill retorted, "Not at all . . . . If Hitler invaded Hell I would make at least a favourable reference to the Devil in the House of Commons." Nor did Churchill try to sup with the Russian devil with a long spoon. The Royal Navy and merchant fleet were to carry vital supplies right into Russia's Arctic ports, at enormous cost in both life and treasure. True, there came a time after 1944 . when Stalin was beginning to show himself a real devil, and the West was in need of the longest possible spoon. But if Churchill failed then to react adequately, he was not the only one. Later, he was, in fact, the first to see the danger.

Churchill made his first visit to Roosevelt in August, 1941. The meeting took place at Placentia Bay, Newfoundland, where the "astonishing" (again Churchill's word) Atlantic Charter was drafted. Churchill was deeply impressed that a non-belligerent like America should join with a belligerent like Britain, if only in enunciating the principles for future, rather than present, peace and security. He was careful to refer to the Charter as a "star" rather than a "law."

Russia and America, however, were not Churchill's only pre-occupations during this summer. He had set his heart on driving Rommel out of North Africa—a controversial strategy. Should he perhaps have regarded the defence of the Far East rather than of the Near East as his paramount duty, second only to the defence of the Island? However that may be, it was the Far East which next exploded.

PEARL HARBOR

On December 7, 1941, the Japanese fell upon the American Pacific Fleet lying at Pearl Harbor in Hawaii. The attack was a complete surprise. Out of eight American battleships present, four were sunk, four badly damaged. The psychological blow to America was no less severe. Instantaneous, violent anger blazed up, sweeping Roosevelt and his country straight into the white-hot heart of the war. By attacking America, the Japanese caused their Axis ally, Hitler, to come into the war against America also.

Churchill happened to be giving dinner at Chequers to the American ambassador, John G. Winant, and his friend Averell Harriman, when the first jumbled intimations of Pearl Harbor came through on the nine o'clock news. Churchill immediately telephoned Roosevelt. "Mr. President, what's this about Japan?" "It's quite true," replied the most important voice in the world. "They have attacked us at Pearl Harbor. We are all in the same boat now." Churchill handed the telephone to Winant, noting the "admirable fortitude" with which the two distinguished Americans took the blow. He himself felt no compunction about facing the tremendous new situation squarely. He got on to Roosevelt again and said: "This certainly simplifies things. God be with you."

God was at any rate with Britain. From now on there could be only one outcome to the Second World War—defeat for the three Axis powers. That great connoisseur of events, Winston Churchill, had heard of Pearl Harbor with a gasp and was to describe it with bated breath. It constituted without doubt "the supreme world event."

On December 8, both Houses of Parliament voted unanimous approval of the declaration of war on Japan, after Churchill had made one of his eloquent speeches. "In the past we have had a light which flickered, in the present we have a light which flames, and in the future there will be a light which shines over all the land and sea."

His note advising the Japanese ambassador that a state of war existed between their two countries was considered by some people almost too eloquent. It ended with the words, "I have the honour to be, with high consideration, Sir, Your obedient servant, Winston S. Churchill." The ceremonious penman replied to critics with typical good humour: "But after all when you have to kill a man it costs nothing to be polite."

Churchill now knew that the Allied victory which he had consistently predicted was assured. It was just as well. Only three days after Pearl Harbor, Britain's sea power was also grievously smitten by Japan. On December 10, he was in bed opening his boxes. Suddenly the telephone rang. It was the First Sea Lord, his voice sounding odd and broken. "Prime Minister, I have to report to you that the *Prince of Wales* and the *Repulse* have both been sunk by the Japanese—we think by aircraft."

These two great ships—a battleship and a battle cruiser—had been sunk off the Malay Peninsula. The way now lay open for a Japanese conquest hitherto undreamed of by Churchill. "I confess," he wrote, "that in my mind the whole Japanese menace lay in a sinister twilight, compared with our other needs." Defence of the Near East was, of course, one of those other needs. Afterwards, Churchill stoutly maintained that "nothing we could have spared at the time...would have changed the march of fate in Malaya." Though he professed to be "sure" of this, one wonders. He reacted with such terrible agony to the sinking of the two ships that one cannot help asking whether a momentary stab of self-accusation was not added to the rest of his sufferings.

Seven months before the sinkings, the Chief of the Imperial General Staff, General Sir John Dill, had argued that the defence of Singapore must come before Egypt. Churchill had rejected this strategy. Nor did he accept the First Lord's and First Sea Lord's advice that the two ships should not go east without air cover. When the news of the disaster to the *Prince of Wales* and *Repulse* reached him, he felt as if those bombs had scored a direct hit on him personally. "I was thankful to be alone."

It was like a certain traumatic moment six months earlier, only a thousand times worse. Then, in June, 1941, he had gone down to Chartwell "wishing to be alone" when the result of "Operation Battleaxe" came in. "Battleaxe" was General Archibald Wavell's attempt to destroy Rommel's forces in North Africa. It failed, though the British held on to Tobruk. When Churchill heard of the failure, he wandered for hours in the lovely Chartwell valley, solitary and disconsolate.

With the entry of America and Russia into the war, Churchill's position was no longer the same. The Second World War as a whole was undoubtedly the "finest hour" of Churchill's long and splendidly eventful life. But within that war itself, the period of May, 1940, to December, 1941, will rightly be called his finest hour of all. From 1942 until victory three and a half years later, he would no longer be alone. Though he, Roosevelt, and Stalin were technically equal, two of them were more equal than the other. As Liddell Hart puts it, "from that time [1942] onward Churchill inevitably counted less than Roosevelt and Stalin in the conduct of the war, because of the much greater resources they wielded. He became 'President Roosevelt's lieutenant.' "

IMPERIAL WAR MUSEUM

Churchill and his daughter Mary travelling by battleship to the United States in December, 1941, after Pearl Harbor.

This phrase, however, happened to be Churchill's own title for his new status. He adopted it without a trace of rancour; rather, with deep but amused satisfaction. To Churchill it was always the cause which counted.

Moreover, the planning of strategy by the Big Three could be nothing short of thrilling to a mind like Churchill's. The vastly extended horizons, the expanding responsibilities, the increasing complexities of choice and decision, the formidable debates with two immensely powerful Heads of State—all these were a pure intellectual treat. There was never a moment when he longed to be back in the narrower confines of the Island.

His first activity after the British and American sea tragedies of December, 1941, was characteristic. He sped across the Atlantic in H.M.S. *Duke of York* to see the President.

During his eight-day voyage, storm-tossed as he was in all senses, he drafted with the help of his Chiefs of Staff a timetable for the rest of the war. Part I assumed total victory in North and West Africa by 1942; Part II envisaged re-establishment of the Pacific Front; Part III planned a major assault on the Continent in 1943. There was hope of ending the war in 1943 or 1944.

IMPERIAL WAR MUSEUM

IMPERIAL WAR MUSEUM

With the benefit of hindsight, Churchill later described this strategy as optimistic—*dangerously* optimistic. Even if "Operation Torch" (the invasion of North Africa) had gone as smoothly as he hoped in 1942—which it did not—the landing craft and the "Mulberry" (floating) harbours could never have been ready for "Operation Overlord" (the invasion of France, known as the Second Front) in 1943. Therefore, if the major assault on the Continent had in fact opened in 1943, the result, noted Churchill, would have been a "world-shaking disaster." Thus Churchill was to conceive of himself and his Allies as "fortunate in our disappointment." At the same time, his rosy schedule with its Parts I, II, and III, seemed to him in its own way equally fortunate. For it proved to the suspicious Stalin that he did indeed advocate a Second Front in 1943. And so all was for the buoyant best.

CHURCHILL IN THE NEW WORLD

The British party landed at Washington airport on December 22, 1941, and were met by Roosevelt himself. "I clasped his strong hand with comfort and pleasure," wrote Churchill. "I have never seen that fellow in better form," remarked Max Beaverbrook of Churchill to the latter's doctor, Lord Moran, after the first evening's discussion. "He conducted the conversation for two hours with great skill."

In the midst of incessant business—"I do not know how I got through it all"—Churchill found time on Christmas Eve to wish the American crowds a happy Christmas from the President's balcony. "I cannot truthfully say I feel far from home," he said with reference to his mother. On Christmas Day, it was more than a pleasure for Churchill to go to church with the President. And on December 26, he addressed Congress. Winston was again "quite at home." Could he not trace direct descent, through Jennie, from a lieutenant who had served in George Washington's army? There were times when he had felt considerably less at home in the House of Commons. "By the way, I cannot help reflecting," he continued to gusts of laughter, "that if my father had been American and my mother British, instead of the other way round, I might have got here on my own." Congress cheered as if it would never stop when he trounced the Japanese. "What sort of people do they think we are?" Altogether it was not surprising that the invisible wings were beating again. "I had the feeling . . . of being used, however unworthy, in some appointed plan."

Facing page:
Canadian Parliament,
December, 1941. Churchill
won stupendous applause
for his comment on the
Vichy French prediction
that Hitler would wring
the British chicken's neck:
"Some chicken!
Some neck!"

Facing page: On the
observation platform of his
special train during a halt
at a small town station
in Canada.

Churchill had a slight heart attack on the night after his speech to Congress. He sent for Lord Moran, who decided to tell no one. The doctor's reason was convincing: "America has just come into the war, and there is no one but Winston to take her by the hand." This was no moment to tell the American newspapers "that the P.M. was an invalid with a crippled heart and a doubtful future."

After Congress, the Canadian Parliament at Ottawa. This was the occasion when he made public the earlier gloomy predictions of the Vichy French generals: "In three weeks," they had said in June, 1940, "England will have her neck wrung like a chicken." Churchill could now retort gaily, "Some chicken! Some neck!" This, he wrote modestly, went very well.

He had to postpone a speech to the House of Commons. "Utterly impossible to lay another egg so early as the New Year," he cabled Attlee. For there was still the United Nations Pact to be signed at the White House on January 1, 1942. The signatories to this "majestic document" were Roosevelt, Churchill, Maxim Litvinov (for Russia), and T. V. Soong (for China), with 22 other signatures to be collected. "The Declaration could not by itself win battles," wrote Churchill afterwards, "but it set forth who we were and what we were fighting for." At the time, he triumphantly showed Roosevelt the stirring lines on Waterloo from Byron's *Childe Harold,* one of his favourite poems:

> *Here, where the sword United Nations drew,*
> *Our countrymen were warring on that day!*
> *And this is much—and all—which will not pass away.*

One result of the Washington conference which *could* win battles was the establishment of the Combined Chiefs of Staff Committee, which would coordinate all operations of British and American forces. As Churchill later said: "There never was a more serviceable war machinery established among allies."

Churchill left for home on January 15 by flying boat from Bermuda. Typically, he had conceived a romantic attachment to this craft during the flight from Washington. Disregarding the attendant *Duke of York,* he cajoled the flying boat's captain into going the whole hog, *"totus porcus."* Losing their way, they came in from the direction of enemy-occupied France. Four Hurricanes were sent up to shoot them down. "However," related this unrepentant adventurer, "they failed in their mission."

Even if Churchill's new mission for 1942 were merely to continue providing the lion with its roar, he would still need all his courage. In January, the great Rommel began his sweep across Cyrenaica (the eastern province of Libya) from west to east, forcing General Sir Claude Auchinleck to retreat nearly 300 miles. While roaring his defiance in the House of Commons, Churchill could not resist paying a chivalrous tribute to Auchinleck's Desert adversary—"a very daring and skilful opponent." Not everyone was pleased. But Nicolson wrote of this period: "No man but he could tell us of such disaster and increase rather than diminish confidence." Less than three weeks later, Singapore surrendered to the Japanese. This "dark moment" of February 15 again brought forth comfort from Washington. "It gives the well-known back-seat driver a field-day," wrote Roosevelt sympathetically, thinking of all the inevitable critics.

Back-seat drivers could also point to the packs of U-boats in the Atlantic. One pack of 20 sank 15 ships in three days, 12 of them British. Roosevelt told his friend Winston on March 18, 1942, to forget Singapore and the Dutch Indies for the time being; to hold India—"Australia . . . we are willing to undertake that"— and to expect shortly F.D.R.'s plan for a Second Front.

Churchill in the R.A.F. Mess, where he and Mrs. Churchill had tea informally with the officers.

IMPERIAL WAR MUSEUM

151

But it was Stalin in the next two years who was going to assume the lead in demanding ever more insistently a Second Front to reduce the pressure on Russia. Churchill's dilemma of the later war years was taking shape. His duty was to prevent a premature "Overlord" (Second Front) by concentrating the Allied war effort on the Pacific and "Torch" (North Africa). At the same time, this smallest of the Big Three, powerwise, must not give the impression that he, the tail, was wagging the dog: that he was against a confrontation on the Western Front in principle; in fact, that the ghost of Churchill Mark 1915 rode again, resolved at last to have his victorious battles in the Mediterranean, the Balkans, Greece, Crete, even in Gallipoli; that he was willing to undertake anything, anywhere—except another Passchendaele, the awful Western Front campaign which had cost the British a quarter of a million casualties in 1917. Roosevelt's letter of March 18 showed the first signs of a difference of opinion with Churchill. "I know you will not mind my being brutally frank," the President wrote, "when I tell you that I think I can personally handle Stalin better than either your Foreign Office or my State Department. Stalin hates the guts of all your top people. He thinks he likes me better, and I hope he will continue to do so."

There was a smile on the face of the Russian tiger. But as the President was being taken for a ride on its back, he could not see the smile.

This important letter ended with an appeal to Winston to "keep up your optimism and your grand driving force" (despite the two back-seat drivers now in operation). Let Winston take a leaf out of F.D.R.'s notebook. "Once a month I go to Hyde Park [his country home] for four days, crawl into a hole, and pull the hole in after me."

During the rest of that year, there was little chance for Churchill to get into a hole, even for one day. There were frequent "rough and surly" messages from Stalin. A temporary cessation of the ruinous Arctic convoys produced one such. Churchill was forced by the Russian Foreign Minister, Vyacheslav Molotov, to issue a communiqué in June describing a Second Front *now* as "urgent." But he qualified the communiqué by handing Molotov an aide-memoire containing the words, "We can therefore give no promise in the matter." All square again.

At about the same time, Churchill paid his third visit to Roosevelt, to concert strategy. He took with him his Chief of the Imperial General Staff, now Sir Alan Brooke. Roosevelt's father, it appeared, had once entertained Brooke's father. But despite this amenity, the visit was traumatic. A telegram arrived on the morning of June 21. The President handed it to Churchill in silence. It read: "Tobruk has surrendered, with twenty-five thousand men taken prisoners." At Singapore, and now at Tobruk, British armies had surrendered to an inferior number of enemy forces. "Defeat is one thing," Churchill noted; "disgrace is another." But there were no recriminations.

"What can we do to help?" asked Roosevelt at once.

"Give us as many Sherman tanks as you can spare," replied Churchill equally promptly, "and ship them to the Middle East as quickly as possible."

Churchill's doctor, Lord Moran, found his heart going out to this unbeatable man. He wrote in his diary, "There is never any danger of his folding up in dirty weather. . . . I do like a really full-sized man. With our military prestige at zero here, he has dominated the discussion."

Churchill had met for the first time two major generals, Dwight D. Eisenhower and Mark Clark. He was deeply impressed by them. They talked about the cross-Channel invasion, now planned for 1943. The operation was initially called "Round-Up." Churchill disapproved of the code name. "Who will be Rounded Up, the Germans or ourselves?" The name was later changed to "Overlord."

Back home, there was hell to pay in Parliament. A vote of censure on the Government for constant disasters, culminating in Tobruk, was moved by Sir John Wardlaw-Milne early in July. Fortunately for Churchill, one of the eccentric remedies proposed by Sir John was the appointment of the King's brother, Henry Duke of Gloucester, as Commander-in-Chief.

Churchill won a huge vote of confidence—475 to 25. In answer to the congratulations of Roosevelt and Hopkins, he replied to the latter: "Thank you so much, my friend. I knew you and the President would be glad of this domestic victory. I hope one day I shall have something more solid to report."

A FLAMING TORCH

The beginnings of something more solid were seen that August, but, as so often happens, they were heralded by a further tragedy. Setbacks in the Desert demanded radical changes in command to give the Army a sense of a fresh start, and Churchill flew off to Cairo to "settle the decisive questions on the spot." General Sir Harold Alexander was to be Commander-in-Chief Near East, in

Despite the inevitable postponement of the Second Front, first to 1943 and then to 1944, preparations for attack went forward in Britain. Here Churchill watches a Halifax bomber.

place of the luckless Auchinleck. General Sir Bernard Law Montgomery would succeed Alexander in "Torch" and General W. H. E. Gott would command the Eighth Army. But on August 7, Churchill learned that the plane bringing out Gott had been shot down. He thereupon sent to Attlee one of the decisive telegrams of the war, asking for Montgomery to command the Eighth Army. "Pray send him by special plane at earliest moment." On the 8th, Churchill was told that the orders for the transfers had been given. "Rommel, Rommel, Rommel, Rommel!" he cried, striding up and down at the Cairo Embassy. "What else matters but beating him?" Montgomery assumed command of the Desert Army on August 13.

Montgomery for the Eighth Army, with Alexander in supreme command of what was now the Middle East. This was the beginning of victory.

Meanwhile, Churchill had flown off to Moscow, where he broke the news to a "glum Stalin" that there would be no Second Front that year. It was his first meeting with the "great Revolutionary Chief," who in time to come he was occasionally to find genial. On this visit, the pleasantest feature was "the flowing current of the taps" in State Villa No. 7, where he lodged. It is amusing to remember that Churchill's famous predecessor, Wellington, had once visited Russia and afterwards copied their

Churchill at Tel-el-Kebir, August, 1942. Cheering troops lined the road to welcome him during his tour of tank units.

IMPERIAL WAR MUSEUM

154

IMPERIAL WAR MUSEUM

*Churchill with Averell
Harriman, Roosevelt's special
representative in Britain,
inspecting a Guard of Honour
on their arrival in Moscow, 1942.
Molotov is at left. Churchill
drew a crocodile to explain to
Stalin that the "soft underbelly"
of the Axis must be ripped up
before a Second Front
could start.*

method of double-glazing. Churchill was to copy their method of
dispensing with plugs in hand-basins. "If there is no scarcity of
water," he wrote, "it is far the best."

On returning to Cairo, he heard that an audacious and gallant
raid on Dieppe on the coast of Occupied France, carried out
mainly by Canadian forces, had been marred by heavy casualties.
The losses were justified, Churchill said, by the information and
expertise obtained for the future invasion. A cross-Channel operation would require floating harbours; "Overlord" would depend
on "Mulberry."

September and October, 1942, were critical months for Churchill;
indeed, he later told Moran they were the worst of the whole war
though he put on "a bold front." There was so much criticism at
home that Brendan Bracken feared for his friend's political future.

Then in November, 1942, came the turning point. It was to be
a month of Allied victory. On the 4th, Rommel was defeated by
Montgomery's Eighth Army at the great Battle of Alamein. To
Churchill it meant that "the Hinge of Fate" (the title of Volume
IV of his *Second World War*) had turned. He wrote: "It may almost be said, 'Before Alamein we never had a victory. After
Alamein we never had a defeat.'" Or, as Lord Moran was to put
it, "After El Alamein, he was never again in danger of losing his
job as long as the war lasted."

General Alexander wanted all the bells to be rung in Britain.
But Churchill decided to wait till "Torch," now almost alight, had
triumphantly flared up. This was indeed to happen when French
Northwest Africa—Morocco, Algeria, Tunisia—were all invaded
between November 8 and 12.

POPPERFOTO

After leaving Moscow, Churchill stopped in Cairo. Back row (l-r): Air Chief Marshal Sir Arthur Tedder, General Sir Alan Brooke, Admiral Sir H. Harwood, and Mr. R. G. Casey. Front row: Field-Marshal Smuts, Churchill, General Sir Claude Auchinleck, and General Sir Archibald Wavell.

Facing page: The El Alamein campaign— victory in the desert. Top, British artillery in action. Bottom, British trucks under heavy bombardment.

On the 22nd, Stalingrad was finally encircled by Soviet forces and the German General Paulus, with the whole of his Sixth Army, trapped. The besiegers had become the besieged.

It was time for the Big Two to meet again to discuss strategy for 1943—still reckoned the year of destiny.

CASABLANCA AND TEHERAN

The Casablanca Conference in Morocco between Roosevelt, Churchill, and their combined staffs took place in January, 1943. The Conference lasted for a fortnight. Churchill flew out by night in an icy bomber. (He had turned off the heating as it seemed likely to catch fire. Since he never wore pyjamas in his life, he was even worse off than his staff.)

Future plans discussed at Casablanca included the conquest of Tunisia; the bringing forward of Turkey as an eventual ally, for which purpose Churchill was to visit President Inönü at Adana at the end of January; occupation of Sicily and pressure on Italy to divert German forces from Russia; continued bombing of Germany; and finally, a cross-Channel operation, set for August, to secure a limited bridgehead on the Cotentin Peninsula. All this with the object of obtaining Germany's "unconditional surrender."

POPPERFOTO

POPPERFOTO

CONWAY PICTURE LIBRARY

Roosevelt and Churchill in Casablanca, January, 1943, to discuss grand strategy with their Chiefs of Staff.

In many respects, the Casablanca program was obviously a triumph for the Churchillian Mediterranean strategy. Churchill amusingly described how the Conference ended with a shot-gun marriage (i.e., a public handshake) between General de Gaulle and the "liberated" French General Henri Giraud, under the eyes of an astonished press.

Then Churchill swept off the President for a glimpse of beautiful Marrakech, "the Paris of the Sahara." He waved good-bye to the great man from the Marrakech airfield early on the morning of his departure, himself clad only in "my zip, and nothing else except slippers." He crowned this informal four-day holiday by painting his only picture during the war. He painted it, symbolically, from the top of a tower.

Churchill, now 68 years old, arrived home in February thoroughly exhausted. Since Casablanca, he had conferred with Inönü and visited Cyprus, Cairo, and Tripoli. He came down with pneumonia on the 16th. His doctor, Lord Moran, summoned a specialist from Guy's Hospital, Dr. Geoffrey Marshall, who greatly pleased his patient. Pneumonia, said Dr. Marshall, was "the old man's friend." "Why?" "Because it takes them off so quietly." But this young-old man was cured by the new drugs and later fortified by the gift of a live lion from an admirer. He must not forget his roar. Roosevelt, who had also been ill, read in the American press that his friend Winston was "the world's worst patient." He told Winston so, banteringly drawing attention to his own "model" behaviour.

It is true that Winston occasionally flew into rages, but they were short-lived, and Moran defended him lustily in his diary: "I keep my chiding for him who turns his face to the wall, whereas Winston has no intention whatever of dying if sheer will-power will keep him going. Besides, no intelligent man, properly handled, can ever be a bad patient. On the contrary, when Winston is sick he does what he is told, provided, of course, that he is given a good reason."

By March, Churchill was back in form and the Eighth Army back in Tunisia. An operation with the agreeably Churchillian name of "Pugilist" enabled the British to force the Mareth Line. On May 13, General Alexander signalled to Churchill: "The Tunisian campaign is over. . . . We are masters of the North African

RADIO TIMES HULTON PICTURE LIBRARY

The old lion presented with a young lion after recovering from his first attack of pneumonia in February, 1943.

IMPERIAL WAR MUSEUM

Churchill leaving camouflaged quarters where he stayed while visiting Castel Benito and Tripoli, February, 1943.

159

IMPERIAL WAR MUSEUM

The Prime Minister gives the victory sign to sailors and airmen aboard as he disembarks from the ship in which he travelled to the U.S.

shores." Scores of thousands of Germans were scouring the desert for prisoner-of-war cages in which to incarcerate themselves.

Churchill had received the great African news while on his fourth visit to Roosevelt and third to Washington. With May already halfway through, what chance now of "Overlord" in 1943? Churchill's Mediterranean strategy was still to hold the field for another six months. The President, reported Churchill, "felt that everyone was agreed that there was no possibility of a cross-Channel enterprise this year . . . ." This year in fact must be the year of "Husky" (Sicily), which led to the fall of Mussolini. "Overlord" must be carried out "on the largest scale in the spring of 1944."

Since the victory at Tunisia, Churchill had become a hero in Washington. On the drive to F.D.R.'s retreat in the Maryland hills, Churchill's prodigious memory enabled him to expound upon two of his greatest American heroes, Stonewall Jackson and Robert E. Lee, and to recite the whole of the American Civil War poem *Barbara Frietchie*. His American friends riding with him in the car came in loudly with a chorus of "she said."

> *Shoot if you must this old grey head,*
> *But spare your country's flag, SHE SAID.*

160

This tour de force was followed by his second address to Congress. His theme was "One Continent Redeemed." This speech was broadcast to the world. His photograph, mouth close to the microphone, half-moon reading glasses well down his nose, finger raised, expression amiable, spotted bow tie alert, today adorns a handbook on the United States Capitol entitled *We, the People.*

It was thrilling to fly straight from Washington to North Africa and to motor about the liberated countryside, inspecting the victorious troops. "There is no doubt," Churchill decided, "that people like winning very much."

The appointment of Lord Louis Mountbatten to Southeast Asia Command in August during the "Quadrant" Conference in Quebec—followed by another Churchillian broadcast—maintained the spirit of progress. September saw the invasion of Italy's toe by the Allies, and more than Churchill's toe inside the Council Room of the White House. On the 11th, while Roosevelt was pulling the hole in after him at Hyde Park, Churchill presided over a meeting in the White House to discuss the Italian campaign. Present were American war chiefs, and civilians such as

POPPERFOTO

Churchill's
second address to
Congress.

In North Africa
with (l-r) Eisenhower,
Tedder, Marshall,
Montgomery.

IMPERIAL WAR MUSEUM

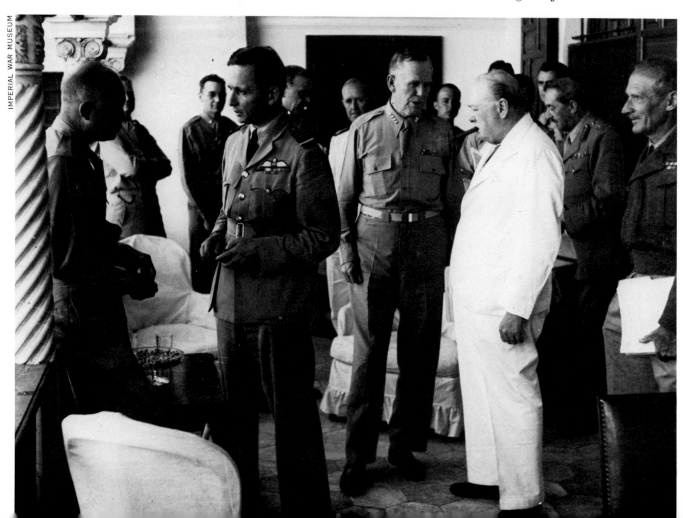

FOX PHOTOS

Churchill responds gaily to cheering crowds.

Hopkins, Harriman, and Lew Douglas, and Churchill's own Chiefs of Staff. Churchill called it "an event in Anglo-American history."

But the future programme was to be what Roosevelt called "British-Russian-United States collaboration." And for Churchill, some of the joy would go out of it.

President Roosevelt was not very well. "It is a nuisenza to have the influenza," he had confided to Churchill towards the end of October. Churchill himself was wretchedly sensitive to the inoculations necessitated by foreign travel. Nevertheless, the preliminaries to the Teheran Conference—the first meeting of the Big Three—were not unsatisfactory. Churchill and the President met first at Cairo, where they celebrated Thanksgiving Day, November 25, with two huge turkeys carved by Roosevelt. There was dancing to a gramophone. As Churchill's daughter Sarah was the only woman present, Churchill himself danced with dear old General Edward ("Pa") Watson, Roosevelt's aide.

The arrival at Teheran was less gay. Security from the airport to the British Legation was nil. "I grinned at the [Persian] crowd," wrote Churchill, "and on the whole they grinned at me." Sarah was more than thankful when they reached their destination safely.

Churchill's malaise from his inoculations had quickly developed into a cold and vicious sore throat. "However, Lord Moran with sprays and ceaseless care enabled me to say what I had to say—which was a lot."

A lot. But not enough to convince his two allies. November, 1943, was to culminate in a series of no, no, noes.

Churchill proposed a three-pronged attack on the Axis. First, "Overlord" in May, June, or early July, 1944. This, the much-postponed Second Front, was by now being planned in all its details. Second, Italy: capture of Rome, followed by stabilisation of the Italian front. After this, Churchill wished the Allies to advance northeastwards through Yugoslavia's Ljubljana Gap, towards Vienna. Roosevelt, on the contrary, preferred a landing along the Riviera. Third, the Eastern Mediterranean: Churchill wanted a tenth—only one little tenth! he argued—of the Allied forces to assist Turkey into the war, perhaps by capturing Rhodes.

Alas, mention of Vienna and Turkey immediately convinced the Americans that here was the old Churchill, off on his Balkan hobby-horse yet again. Stalin also opposed Churchill's Turkish project. He had his own eye on Eastern Europe. Churchill's plans for Eastern Europe were further complicated by the question of "Overlord's" date. They might delay it beyond the now sacred date of May 1, 1944.

Before the second plenary session began, there was a break for the presentation to Stalin of a Sword of Honour from King George VI, in memory of the defence of Stalingrad. Churchill has described the scene with a touch of vinegar which aptly recalls the whole Teheran atmosphere. "When, after a few sentences of explanation, I handed the splendid weapon to Marshal Stalin, he raised it in a most impressive gesture to his lips, and kissed the blade. He then passed it to Voroshilov, who dropped it."

By the end of that second session, it was clear that Stalin, despite the Sword, doubted Churchill's commitment to the Second Front. Looking directly at him across the table, Stalin said: "I

August, 1943. Churchill and daughter Mary visit Niagara Falls in Canada. Churchill remarked that he first visited the Falls in 1900.

IMPERIAL WAR MUSEUM

163

IMPERIAL WAR MUSEUM

IMPERIAL WAR MUSEUM

Churchill at Harvard University, October, 1943. Left, he addresses assembled Army and Navy cadets. Right, arriving at Sanders Theatre to receive an honorary degree. Here, Churchill broached the idea of common Anglo-American citizenship.

wish to pose a very direct question to the Prime Minister about 'Overlord.' Do the Prime Minister and the British Staff really believe in 'Overlord'?"

It was the most effective way possible of driving a wedge between Churchill and Roosevelt. Once he had got going, Stalin was to add to his own pleasure by teasing as well as taunting Churchill. At one point, he insisted that 50,000 German officers and technicians must be shot after the Allied victory. Churchill marched out of the room, furiously muttering remarks about "infamy" and "sullying his country's honour." Stalin brought him back with a clap on the shoulder and a broad grin. It was all a joke—or so he said.

Hitherto, Churchill's strategy, as we have seen, had been accepted by his American allies. The Teheran Conference changed all that. When the main points were decided, they were not in accordance with Churchill's wishes. Roosevelt, it seemed, was being mesmerised by Stalin's siren songs.

No operation was to be allowed which might delay "Overlord" beyond May 1; Churchill would have preferred the date of "Overlord" to be July. The soft underbelly of the Axis was to be, not the Ljubljana Gap, but the south of France ("Operation Anvil"). This, combined with "Overlord," was to have priority over Churchill's Mediterranean strategy and the forthcoming Italian campaign. And a defeated Germany was to be partitioned into smaller units than Churchill thought desirable or realistic.

It was curious how so many of the code names seemed to fit. With the fall of Tunis, "Torch" had indeed proven a dazzler. The last Washington conference had been called "Trident," as though to mark the fact that Britannia's shield and trident were still well to the fore. But "Anvil" marked the influence of Russia, with Churchill hammered, however gently, between Stalin and Roosevelt. After that the code names did not fit so well. Whoever thought of calling the Teheran Conference "Eureka"?

JOHN COLVILLE, CB, CVO

Winston and Clemmie at Marrakech, after a picnic.

Churchill's 69th birthday was celebrated at Teheran by a splendid dinner. He wrote: "On my right sat the President of the United States, on my left the master of Russia." The Prime Minister of Britain felt well satisfied with his own constitutional position. "They could order; I had to convince and persuade: I was glad that this should be so."

After the Conference was over, Churchill met Inönü again in Cairo. "The President of the Turks kissed me—twice," he told Sarah afterwards. "The trouble with me is that I am irresistible." He also met Roosevelt in Cairo to discuss the High Command for "Overlord." Contrary to Churchill's expectations, General Eisenhower was to command in France and General George C. Marshall to remain in Washington, not vice versa. "I feel I could not sleep at night," the President had said to Marshall, "with you out of the country."

Churchill insisted that his friend look at the Sphinx before they all parted on December 7. "Roosevelt and I gazed at her for some minutes in silence as the evening shadows fell. She told us nothing and maintained her inscrutable smile."

Just like Stalin.

CLOSING IN

Suddenly Churchill felt extraordinarily tired. He was due to fly on to Alexander's and Montgomery's Headquarters in Italy after spending a night at Carthage with Eisenhower. But Ike met a collapsed Churchill at the Tunis airfield. "I am completely at the end of my tether, and I cannot go on to the front until I have recovered some strength." He slept all that day in Ike's hospitable villa. Next day he had pneumonia. "So here I was at this pregnant moment on the broad of my back amid the ruins of ancient Carthage." Was he not something of an ancient ruin himself? Certainly not. He went through his red boxes, in defiance of doctor's orders. ("In defeat, defiance.") He had the wit to christen the new drug M & B which saved his life "Moran and Bedford," the names of his two doctors. Clementine, Jock Colville, and Beaverbrook flew out to be with him, and Sarah read *Pride and Prejudice* aloud. He thought Jane Austen's calm went very well with M & B.

It would be rash to underestimate the severity of Churchill's illnesses during the war, especially in view of his doctor's statements. "It was exhaustion of mind and body," wrote Lord Moran in *Winston Churchill: The Struggle For Survival, 1940–1965*, "that accounts for much that is otherwise inexplicable in the last years of the war—for instance, the deterioration of his relations with Roosevelt." But this is surely going too far. Churchill's deteriorating position vis-à-vis Roosevelt and Stalin was fully accounted for by the change in the balance of international power. Churchill's own staff make the point most effectively in *Action This Day*. Perhaps the most that should be said is that during the last year of the war, Churchill carried the marks of one heart attack and two bouts of pneumonia, as well as all his other burdens. More honour to him.

By Christmas Day, he was holding a key conference at Carthage with American and British Chiefs of Staff. It concerned the Italian campaign as it affected "Overlord."

The landings at Anzio, southeast of Rome, would not be ready to begin until January 20, 1944. Anzio would require the use of 56 landing craft scheduled for "Overlord," and due to be

Exhausted after Teheran, Churchill fell ill with pneumonia at Carthage, where Eisenhower succoured him. Ike gave a luncheon on Christmas Day, 1943, in honour of his friend's recovery. General Alexander stands behind Ike and Winston in his bedragoned dressing gown.

IMPERIAL WAR MUSEUM

POPPERFOTO

In the amphitheatre of ancient Carthage.

sent back to England a week or so before that date. Churchill now proposed delaying the return of these landing craft until February 5. This in turn would mean delaying "Overlord" till the end of May—or even "around 6 June," when the moon would be right. Of course, the preliminary bombardment of German installations would begin in May. But would Roosevelt feel that this fulfilled the Teheran "contract"?

Churchill was ecstatic when Roosevelt agreed to the landing craft being detained for use at Anzio, but Anzio alone. "I cannot agree without Stalin's approval," Roosevelt telegraphed, "to any use of forces or equipment elsewhere that might delay or hazard the success of 'Overlord' or 'Anvil.'" Though Roosevelt's decision meant jettisoning the East Mediterranean and also a project in West Burma, it was more than Churchill had dared to hope for. He wired back: "I thank God for this fine decision, which engages us once again in wholehearted unity upon a great enterprise."

The irony was that Anzio proved to be a heroic anti-climax. "I intended to throw ashore a hell-cat," he told Jock Colville, "and all I got was an old stranded whale." Years later, on being questioned by Moran, Churchill named Anzio as his worst moment of the war.

JOHN COLVILLE, CB, CVO

Churchill concludes a successful speech. These are some of the troops who were to invade Europe in the summer of 1944.

With breathless absorption, Churchill followed the exciting events in many theatres of war. Josip Tito and his partisans were successful in Yugoslavia. Alexander's forces drew off many German divisions into southern Italy. The Burma campaign was running its remarkable course, and by June 22, Mountbatten was able to report to Churchill that "the road to the plain was open." Mountbatten had had exactly a week and a half of supplies and ammunition left. Now suddenly the convoys were rolling in.

Meanwhile, Rome had been taken on June 4 amid universal applause—"I even got a pat from the Bear," wrote Churchill—and, two days later, "Operation Overlord" had begun.

FROM D DAY TO V-E DAY

It was once said of Churchill by his friend Lord Birkenhead: "No one Department, hardly one war, was enough for him." When the climax of the Second World War was only a matter of days away, the truth of this remark again became apparent. To inspire the war effort, to direct the war, to confer with generals, admirals, and statesmen, all these things were not enough for Churchill. Shortly before D Day, the old longing which had come over him at Antwerp in 1914 to be an integral part of the battle once more possessed him. He planned to go in with the troops, on board the Admiral's flagship.

168

Unfortunately for him, there was another character at the head of Britain's affairs as romantic and nostalgic as himself. When the sailor-king George VI heard of Churchill's plan, he decided to go too. This was more than the Establishment could bear. The King was persuaded to renounce the adventure. He in turn hoped that Churchill would do likewise. "I must defer to your Majesty's wishes, and indeed command," replied the reluctant Prime Minister from Southampton on June 3, where he was already waiting, so to speak, with steam up. Three days later, the armada sailed without him. He could not resist pointing out in 1952 that "the cruiser squadron concerned was, as I had justly estimated, not exposed to any undue danger." In the safe knowledge of this fact, posterity may be forgiven for wishing that among the 4,000 ships and 11,000 first-line aircraft assembled for D Day, and the 150,000 troops embarked for the first wave of attacks, there had been both the King and Prime Minister of Britain.

Rough weather had brought about a final, last-minute postponement of D Day from the 5th to the 6th of June. Despite this contretemps, the invasion went forward as a miracle of precision on the Allies' part and an utter surprise to the Germans. They had written it off as soon as the wind rose.

Eisenhower's careful statement in his *Crusade in Europe* contrasts amusingly with Churchill's flamboyance in the House of Commons, both of them describing the first morning's work. "As the morning wore on," wrote Eisenhower, "it became apparent that the landing was going fairly well." Churchill, after playfully keeping the Commons on tenterhooks by a short dissertation on the Italian campaign, suddenly plunged into the D Day story: "I have also to announce to the House that during the night and the early hours of this morning the first of the series of landings in force upon the European Continent has taken place. . . . So far the commanders who are engaged report that everything is proceeding according to plan. And what a plan! This vast operation . . . tides, winds, waves, visibility . . . combined employment of land, air, and sea forces in the highest degree of intimacy and in contact with conditions which could not and cannot be fully foreseen. . . . Complete unity prevails throughout the Allied Armies. There is a brotherhood in arms between us and our friends of the United States. . . . complete confidence . . . Eisenhower . . . Montgomery . . . ardour and spirit . . . equipment, science . . . forethought . . . utmost resolution . . . ."

POPPERFOTO

Above: British troops land in Italy, September, 1943. The early stages of this campaign gave Churchill his worst moment of the war. Right: British troops go ashore in France as the invasion is at last under way, June, 1944. To his great regret, Churchill could not view the June 6 assault from the Admiral's flagship.

POPPERFOTO

POPPERFOTO

Above: D Day landings by American troops. Left: On his way to the Normandy beaches in Admiral Vian's barge, Churchill manages a D Day of his own.

POPPERFOTO

The great Churchillian periods rolled forward much as the D Day forces were at that moment rolling up the five Normandy beaches, with their splendidly romantic names—Utah, Omaha, Gold, Juno, Sword. And the great Churchillian concepts of unity and brotherhood descended on the House much as the parachutes were descending behind the beaches in airborne landings.

Churchill managed a D Day of his own on June 10. Montgomery met him on the beach as he landed from a British destroyer. They lunched at "Monty's" H.Q., five miles inland. Churchill admired the lovely red and white cows "parading" in the sunshine. After visiting local ports and watching from Admiral Vian's *Kelvin* the Allied battle cruisers bombarding the German shore batteries, they turned to go. "Since we are so near," said the irrepressible Churchill suddenly, "why shouldn't we have a plug at them ourselves before we go home?" "Certainly," said Vian. He fired a salvo and then made off at high speed, out of harm's way. Churchill rightly paid tribute to the Admiral's "sporting spirit," having much enjoyed the new sensation of being on board a ship which was firing shots in anger. Roosevelt was then given an account of this "jolly day" with its concluding "plug at the Hun."

Three days later, "the Hun" had a plug at England. This plug was to be far more damaging and protracted. The first of the pilotless aircraft—the V-1, or "vengeance weapon"—arrived over England and dropped their bombs. With what can only be described as "fearful symmetry," the Guards Chapel in the heart of London was destroyed on June 18, Waterloo Day. Eisenhower believed that if the Germans' V-1s and later V-2s had been ready earlier and had bombed, say, Southampton, they could have put an end to D Day before it began.

A month later, Churchill was visiting Utah Beach in a British motor torpedo-boat. He watched the miracle of the D.U.K.W.s (amphibious vehicles) "swimming" through the harbour, "waddling" ashore, as he put it, and carrying their supplies on up the hill to waiting trucks. At night, a sing-song in the wardroom produced the chorus of *Rule Britannia*. Did the officers know the words? asked Churchill. They did not. So he was able to celebrate another triumph similar to the recitation in America of *Barbara Frietchie*. British sailors were taught *Rule Britannia*:

> *The nations not so blest as thee*
> *Must in their turn to tyrants fall:*
> *While thou shalt flourish great and free,*
> *The dread and envy of them all.*

JOHN COLVILLE, CB, CVO

Churchill meets the handsome Marshal Tito of Yugoslavia at Caserta in August, 1944. Churchill was glad to be in cooler, if less grand, attire than Tito.

Following the planned sequence of the invasion—"Lodgment, Breakout, Pursuit"—the troops poured through summer France. Paris was liberated on August 25, with De Gaulle giving thanks in a cathedral still crackling sporadically with collaborators' bullets. "In September our armies were crowding up against the borders of Germany," wrote Eisenhower. By the 9th of that month, one source of England's recent hell—the flying-bomb launching sites—had been overrun, and what the British called doodle-bugs or buzz bombs gradually ceased, though the dreadful silent rockets (V-2s) continued to take their toll until March, 1945.

Meanwhile, Churchill had been south to Italy, where he wished to discuss politics with Marshal Tito of Yugoslavia, before "Anvil" (now renamed "Dragoon") began on the Riviera. They met at Naples on August 12 in full view of Vesuvius. Tito seemed to be quite as hot as the volcano, but this was because he honoured his host by wearing a spectacular blue and gold uniform presented by the Russians, with the lace added by the Americans. The collar was too tight for such heat. Churchill called it a "gold-lace strait-jacket" and was thankful to be in white ducks himself.

After that, Churchill flew off to Corsica, to watch the "Anvil-Dragoon" landings taking place on the coast of France opposite. He was deeply anxious about the consequences.

IMPERIAL WAR MUSEUM

Churchill watching the progress of "Anvil-Dragoon." Though he had disapproved of the strategy of the Riviera landings, he wished the operation "all success.... indeed, I thought it was a good thing I was near the scene to show the interest I took in it."

Earlier in August, Churchill had tried in vain to divert "Anvil" to the west coast of France, where the forces could quickly join with "Overlord." He tackled both Roosevelt and Hopkins by wire, and Eisenhower in person. Hopkins defended the operation using a striking word: the southern French would "abyssiniate" large numbers of Germans, and "Anvil" would join up with "Overlord" soon enough. Roosevelt was irrevocably opposed to upsetting the "grand strategy" agreed upon at Teheran. Eisenhower proved equally immovable. So it was with typical magnanimity that Churchill decided to give the operation his personal blessing. He watched its opening from a naval vessel. Afterwards he wrote: "I had at least done the civil to 'Anvil.'" But he felt the price had been heavy for the West. "The army of Italy was deprived of its opportunity to strike a most formidable blow at the German," he said, "and very possibly to reach Vienna before the Russians, with all that might have followed therefrom."

There was an alternative to "abyssiniating" the Germans. Why not "pastoralise" them? Their militarism depended on heavy industry. Why not lighten them—and the world—of that load by forcing them after the war to turn their factories into barns and their tanks into tractors? The second Quebec Conference (September,

174

1944) discussed this plan, propounded by Henry Morgenthau, and seriously considered by Roosevelt. Churchill's first instinct was "violently" against it. But as usual in these times, he bowed to his American ally, not to mention his own adviser, Professor Lindemann. He was far from distressed when the Morgenthau plan was eventually discarded, thanks to Foreign Secretary Eden and Secretary of State Cordell Hull.

The German armies were being driven back on all fronts. And now a knock-out blow against Japan must be concerted. To bring Japan to its knees as soon as possible after Germany's defeat, Russia must be persuaded to intervene in the Far East war. The future world organisation of peace which had been discussed at Dumbarton Oaks must also have Russia's participation. Here were two vital reasons for another meeting with Stalin. Since F.D.R. was fully occupied with his fourth presidential election, due on November 7, Churchill flew off without him to see "U.J." ("Uncle Joe"), arriving in Moscow on October 9, 1944.

Despite his deep suspicions of international communism, Churchill always felt he got on well man to man with Uncle Joe. He had no objections to Russian feasts and late hours, unlike his colleagues, since he kept late hours himself. He and Stalin stood side by side in the Royal Box at the Bolshoi Ballet while "an almost passionate demonstration" of loyalty surged around them. That was on the 14th. The previous day was later described by Churchill as "All Poles' Day" because of protracted discussions

Below: Churchill in two of his many hats. At left, he confers with Smuts in the garden of the Cairo Embassy, 1942. At right, greeting F.D.R. at Quebec, 1944. The press called this "a happy picture," but Churchill's doctor spotted the sad deterioration in the President's health: "You could have put your fist between his neck and his collar."

IMPERIAL WAR MUSEUM

IMPERIAL WAR MUSEUM

POPPERFOTO

*A Thanksgiving Day
Tribute to America, 1944.
Harold Nicolson described
Churchill at this date as
"cherubic, pink, solid
and vociferous."*

with the two groups of Polish fighters—the Free Poles of London and the Lublin, or Communist, Poles. The latter, Churchill realised, were the mere tools of Moscow. "I cross-examined them fairly sharply," he wrote to King George VI, "and on several points Marshal Stalin backed me up." Judging by the final and inevitable outcome of a Communist Poland, perhaps a better name for the occasion would have been "All Fools' Day"—except, of course, that Stalin was a villain but no fool.

Churchill had nonetheless tried manfully to retain some hold on the plans for Eastern Europe after the war. At his first meeting with Stalin (October 9), he had drafted a table showing the degree of "influence" to be enjoyed in various Balkan countries by Russia and "Others." He pushed the paper across to the Russian dictator. Russia was to enjoy 90 percent predominance in Romania, 75 percent in Bulgaria, 50 percent in Yugoslavia and Hungary, and 10 percent in Greece. After reading the list, Stalin took his blue pencil and gave it a huge tick. "It was all settled," wrote Churchill, "in no more time than it takes to set down."

And all except the Greek agreement broken again nearly as quickly. But for Churchill himself, every country on that list (bar the special case of Yugoslavia) would eventually have yielded to 100 percent Russian dominance. On an icy Christmas Eve, 1944, Churchill made a dash to Athens. The whole American and British Left were strongly antipathetic to British intervention in the factional struggle which had broken out in Greece following the collapse of German forces in October. Churchill had never felt more alone in his life. "But if the powers of evil prevail in Greece, as is quite likely," he wrote, "we must be prepared for a quasi Bolshevised Russian-led Balkan Peninsula, and this may spread to Italy and Hungary." When Churchill arrived in Athens, the atmosphere was of snipers, hurricane lamps, and armoured cars. His courageous initiative resulted in the establishment of a temporary regency and prevented a take-over by the Greek Communist forces, unsupported as they were by Stalin. About to be gorged with the countries of Eastern Europe, Stalin was willing to observe the blue pencil tick he had put to Greece. If Churchill did not exclude all "the powers of evil," whether of Left or Right, from Greece forever, at least he preserved an intermittent hope for democracy.

He also preserved the memory of an Anglo-Greek incident which seems to belong to one of Byron's poetic fantasies. On Christmas night, Churchill had invited the future Regent, Archbishop Damaskinos, to meet him for talks on board H.M.S. *Ajax*.

POPPERFOTO/CONWAY PICTURE LIBRARY

Churchill with De Gaulle at an Armistice Day parade in recently liberated Paris, November, 1944. Churchill no longer felt, as he had once said, that "The heaviest cross I have to bear is the Cross of Lorraine."

When he arrived, the sailors were in fancy dress and mistook the towering figure of Damaskinos in archiepiscopal hat and robes for a member of their own Christmas show. They danced mockingly round him to his intense surprise. Wherever Churchill went, it seemed, there tended to be "a sound of revelry by night."

177

THE MANSELL COLLECTION

*Churchill with
Archbishop Damaskinos
in Athens, December,
1944. Eden, in the photo
at right, accompanied
Churchill on his journey
to avert a communist
take-over in
Greece.*

IMPERIAL WAR MUSEUM

U.S. SIGNAL CORPS

In telling his great war story, Churchill was now entering upon the second half of his sixth and last volume. He called this "The Iron Curtain," which explains the note of warning in the title for Volume VI as a whole: *Triumph and Tragedy.*

The concept of an iron curtain, however, had not yet arisen, nor the term been popularised when the Big Three met in order to continue the planning of peace. Churchill and Roosevelt set off in February, 1945, for the Yalta Conference in the Crimea; for each it was a last ever visit to Russia, and for the President a last conference.

Roosevelt had been re-elected President by an impressive majority. Sick but steadfast, he now wanted to make sure of Stalin's cooperation while he still had time. Churchill, ebullient despite his 70 years, swept away any objections to another Big Three meeting. The meeting was named "Argonaut," in memory of the mythical heroes who once sailed to the Crimea.

The conference at Yalta on world organisation was to open in early February and to last only for six days, which Churchill considered rather few. "Even the Almighty took seven," he wrote to F.D.R. Therefore, preliminaries were essential, and he arranged to meet the President first at Malta. The President received a cheerful jingle from his friend on New Year's Day: "No more let us falter! From Malta to Yalta! Let nobody alter!" Nobody did; and the Big Two and their staffs duly arrived in Malta.

From Malta they flew to the Crimea, landing on the snowy airfield of Saki. Churchill now noted how "frail" F.D.R. looked. Lord Moran, with his doctor's eye, chose even more ominous words to describe the President: muffled in his cape, he looked "old and thin and drawn . . . shrunken."

Churchill salutes as the U.S. warship carrying F.D.R. arrives at Malta. Churchill had written encouragingly to his friend: "No more let us falter! From Malta to Yalta! Let nobody alter!"

179

A drive of some eight hours took them from bleak Saki to sunny Yalta. Churchill's party, including Sarah, had refreshed themselves with sandwiches, only to find awaiting them en route a magnificent luncheon of caviar, smoked salmon, suckling pig, and sweet champagne. The valiant Prime Minister alone was able to do it justice.

At Yalta, they were housed in the stately homes of nineteenth century Russian princes—a Vorontzov, a Yusopov, Tsar Nicholas II himself. While the Big Three worked out their plans for post-war peace-keeping in scenes of palatial splendour, their underlings attempted to deal with the "enemy" which disturbed their peace at night: bedbugs. Though Churchill did not complain in his book, we know from Lord Moran that he was bitten on the feet.

As the few days of Yalta slipped by, Churchill became more and more conscious of Roosevelt's failing powers. Despite the familiar, captivating smile, "his face had a transparency, an air of purification" and his eyes "a far-away look." He nevertheless seemed to have achieved his goal. He had got Stalin working with the two democracies for world peace.

Stalin, for his part, could afford to show particularly warm appreciation of Churchill, the odd man out. He toasted the Prime Minister in words which only the most iron-hearted would not have found moving. "To the health of the man who is born once in a hundred years, and who bravely held up the banner of Great Britain." Stalin even mentioned the British Empire in his toast, whereas to Roosevelt it was always anathema. Moran wrote in his diary on February 9: "He [the President] cannot leave the Empire alone. It seems to upset him, though he never turns a hair when a great chunk of Europe falls into the clutches of the Soviet Union." This was amply true of the disposal of Poland at Yalta.

And so the Big Three parted: Roosevelt hoping to build a fairer future with "the Bear" and regretful that "this brave new world stuff" did not appeal to Churchill; Stalin the genial deceiver; Churchill, under no illusions, but tied hand and foot by the continuing war. "What would have happened," he asked afterwards, "if we had quarrelled with Russia while the Germans still had two or three hundred divisions on the fighting front?"

That March, the German divisions were put to the final test. The First Canadian, Second British and Ninth U.S. Armies, all under Montgomery, crossed the Rhine north of the Ruhr on the 24th. Churchill had insisted on a front seat this time. He dined the night before in Monty's caravan (bed for once at 10:00 p.m. sharp). Next morning, he watched the fly-in from the top of a hill

CONWAY PICTURE LIBRARY

The Yalta Conference, February, 1945. Left, Churchill arrives at a meeting, looking his bulldog self. Below, with Molotov and Roosevelt. Churchill noticed the "far-away look" in the President's eyes with deep sorrow.

POPPERFOTO

JOHN COLVILLE, CB, CVO

IMPERIAL WAR MUSEUM

*"Operation Plunder."
With Eisenhower,
Churchill watches the
progress of the Rhine
crossing; he later crossed
the Rhine himself, in an
American craft.*

and the assault forces from an armoured car. On the 25th, Churchill himself crossed the Rhine while visiting Eisenhower. The First and Third U.S. Armies under General Omar Bradley crossed south of the Ruhr, and the Seventh U.S. and First French Armies under General J. L. Devers swept across the Rhine farther south. The Ruhr was encircled. The month of April had begun. It was to be a devastating month.

At the beginning of April, there were still no changes among the five leaders who had carried their countries, one way or another, into the Second World War. Roosevelt, Churchill, Stalin, Hitler, and Mussolini were all in the land of the living. True, Mussolini's Italy was defeated and Hitler's Germany about to collapse. The so-called spirit of Yalta, as it affected liberated Poland, had been strangled by Stalin, and quarrels over the terms of German surrender had wrecked the Big Three as a united trinity. Nevertheless, world leadership on both sides still looked the same. In an effort to keep the Big Three together over Poland, F.D.R. telegraphed Churchill on April 12: "I would minimize the general Soviet problem as much as possible . . . . We must be firm however, and our course thus far is correct."

182

IMPERIAL WAR MUSEUM

But now Roosevelt's course was run. That very afternoon, April 12, while sitting for his portrait, he died. On April 28, Mussolini and his mistress were executed by Italian partisans. Two days later, on April 30, Hitler shot himself in his bunker, and his wife of a few days, Eva Braun, took poison.

Churchill heard the news of Roosevelt's death early in the morning of Friday the 13th. He described it in words that remind us of his agony over the sinking of the *Repulse* and *Prince of Wales*. "I felt as if I had been struck a physical blow"—as if the blow which had struck down his friend had hit him too. "My relations with this shining personality had played such a large part in the long, terrible years we had worked together. Now they had come to an end . . . ."

The war in Europe had practically come to an end at the same time. But the prizes and punishments of war still remained to be distributed. Berlin could have fallen to the Western Allies. But what of Vienna? There was no chance of getting there before the Russians. That chance had been thrown away, in Churchill's unalterable view, by the decision in favour of the "Anvil-Dragoon" landings on the Riviera. As for Prague, which Churchill hoped against hope might fall to the United States, it too was entered by the Russians, on May 9. Churchill had written to President Tru-

Another view for the Prime Minister of the Rhine assault, from an armoured car.

183

FOX PHOTOS

V-E Day on the Palace Balcony. Churchill, a dedicated monarchist, once said that when there is victory the King is cheered, when there is defeat the Government falls.

A carload of merrymakers celebrate V-E Day in London.

POPPERFOTO

man ten days before: "If the Western Allies play no significant part in Czechoslovakian liberation that country will go the way of Yugoslavia." He was right in his intuition of disaster.

Three days after the occupation of Prague by Soviet troops, he sent Truman a telegram—"the 'Iron Curtain' telegram," as he called it—on which he was content to stake his reputation as a statesman. "I am profoundly concerned with the European situation," he began. The democracies were withdrawing their great armies from the Continent, while Russia . . . ? Churchill answered his question with a cheerless catalogue of anxieties: over Yalta, over Poland, over the Balkans (except Greece), and over Vienna. On the Russian front, "an iron curtain is drawn down . . . ." His long telegram ended: "To sum up, this issue of a settlement with Russia before our strength has gone seems to me to dwarf all others."

A *settlement with Russia* . . . . That was to be the theme of Churchill's post-war years. Meanwhile, there was a victory to be celebrated.

Churchill announces victory from a balcony in Whitehall to a vast crowd.

IMPERIAL WAR MUSEUM

185

POPPERFOTO

All hostilities ceased by midnight on May 8, 1945, the instrument of "unconditional surrender" (or "total victory") having been signed at Reims in France at 2:41 a.m. on the day before. Churchill appeared on the balcony of Buckingham Palace with the King and Queen on V-E Day (Victory in Europe, May 8) to share, however temperately, in the wild jubilations of the country. Ironically, Mrs. Churchill happened to be with Stalin, working for her "Aid to Russia" scheme.

In retrospect, Churchill remembered his heart as having been heavy on that day of rejoicing. Certainly his broadcast had its sombre moments. If he did not actually spell out "tears, toil, and sweat" (leaving out the blood) as he had five years earlier, he did warn the people that their toils and troubles were not over.

He wound up nonetheless on a gloriously Churchillian note: "Forward unflinching, unswerving, indomitable, till the whole task is done and the whole world is safe and clean."

For a little while longer, it was still his finest hour.

Churchill on V-E Day. His grim expression was an essential part of his mood. The future would not be easy. With Germany devastated and Poland Sovietised, what stood between "the white snows of Russia and the white cliffs of Dover"?

187

"For Valour"

He is the most honored and honorable man to walk the stage of human history in the time in which we live.

PRESIDENT JOHN F. KENNEDY ON CHURCHILL, 1963

FOX PHOTOS

One day at Yalta, Churchill had said, "Stalin and the President can do what they like, whereas in a few months time I may find myself in the street." He was thinking of an upcoming British general election. Stalin, as dictator, was immovable. The allotted span of Roosevelt's fourth presidency would be curtailed only by his death. But a British prime minister was in a very different position. This Parliament was already the longest in British history, running ten years, as against the constitutional limit of five years in normal times. There was bound to be a new Parliament when the war ended. Not that Churchill really expected to be beaten. But it was possible. Thus his remark, "In a few months time I may find myself in the street."

In the street he was, by July 26, 1945, when the election results were announced.

The shock was extreme, since Churchill's personal campaign had seemed to be one long triumph. Those who came to watch his nationwide motorcades during the election came only to cheer. Perhaps this deceived him and his party managers. Afterwards, people said it was all Max Beaverbrook's fault. He had given his friend the wrong advice, encouraging him to roll out the barrels of old-fashioned invective when the nation was waiting for something constructive and new. Moreover, Churchill's picture of the Labour party owed a little too much to his imagination. In his best election snarl he compared it with "the Gestapo." His jokes about its leader "poor Clem" (Attlee), though good-tempered, were a travesty in the other direction: "A sheep in sheep's clothing," he had once said; and in explanation of Attlee's never going abroad, "When the mouse is away the cats will play." Yet when Colville asked Churchill which of his Labour colleagues he respected most, he replied, "Attlee."

Churchill may have had an inkling of what was going on in the mind of the electorate. Labour had been out of office from 1931–40 and since then in a coalition government. If the people wanted a "brave new world," they might turn to Labour. Churchill had often expressed himself as against "this brave-new-world business."

Facing page: Despite a snowstorm, the crowds queue to see Churchill lying in state at Westminster Hall, January, 1965.

KEYSTONE

Outside Hitler's bunker, Churchill poses on what was thought to be Hitler's chair. Churchill had originally wished to banish Hitler to an island—but not St. Helena, which Churchill thought too good for him.

So he woke up at 5:00 a.m. on July 26, 1945, "with a sharp stab of almost physical pain." A premonitory fear had broken through. With the fear went an agonising realisation of what defeat would mean to him. "All the pressure of great events, on and against which I had mentally so long maintained my 'flying speed,' would cease and I should fall." A future without great events. That would indeed be a black one for Churchill. Refusing to contemplate it, he turned over and went to sleep again.

Somehow he knew what to expect when he woke for the second time at 9:00 a.m. In his famous Map Room, where the Allied advances had once been marked up, sweeping Labour victories were now being plotted. A friend said: "But at least, while you held the reins you managed to win the race." "Yes," replied Churchill, with that wonderful humour of his coming to the rescue, "I won the race—and now they have warned me off the turf."

There was one particularly valid reason for Churchill's grievous disappointment. He felt that his work for peace was being left perilously unfinished.

Potsdam, outside Berlin, was the scene during July of the last Summit Conference between the Big Three—Stalin, Truman, and hitherto Churchill. After the general election, the Conference was resumed, but with Attlee now representing Britain. The frontiers between a Sovietised Poland and a dismembered Germany had been, and still were, the subject of vehement debate. Churchill felt that, had things turned out differently, the Americans and he could in the end have beaten down Stalin and saved at least part of East Germany for democracy.

The question of bringing the war against Japan to a victorious close did not particularly worry Churchill. He knew it was only a matter of time. And by a strange coincidence, on the very day that the first plenary session at Potsdam had opened—July 17—he learned of the success of a formidable experiment in the New Mexico desert: "Babies satisfactorily born," the coded message read. In the light of future events, it might seem somewhat cynical to connect the satisfactory birth of babies with that of the atom bomb, even by way of code. The decision to drop the atom bombs on Japan, after the Japanese warlords had rejected unconditional surrender, was taken by Truman, Stalin, and Attlee, but Churchill had already agreed in principle before his fall. V-J Day (Victory over Japan) followed in mid-August, 1945.

Churchill had magnanimously invited Attlee to attend the Potsdam Conference from the beginning, as an observer. In the course of his last banquet there, Churchill had proposed an agreeably loaded toast: "To the Leader of the Opposition—whoever he may be!" Everyone, including Attlee, laughed. They all thought it would be Attlee. But it was to be the proposer of the toast himself.

IMPERIAL WAR MUSEUM

The meeting room for the Potsdam Conference, July, 1945.

Towards the new Parliament, Churchill was the soul of generosity. "The new Government will have terrible tasks," he said. "Terrible tasks. We must do all we can to help them." One M.P. described how Churchill would sit listening to the dullest maiden speeches in order to encourage the beginners. "Never has any man shown such magnanimity. He has recovered all his splendour."

To his doctor, he naturally showed more of the hurt. Sometimes he was "very brave and gentle under the blow," wrote Moran. At other times he was bitter. "If Eisenhower will have me, I think I'll go to the Riviera," he said one day. "I don't mind if I never see England again." But this was not his prevailing mood. (Eisenhower was kindness itself. "I was pleased and honored that he asked me to put him up," he wrote afterwards; "his suggestion implied that he felt for me some little fraction of the great respect, affection, and admiration I had developed for him.") When Moran spoke of the people's "ingratitude," Churchill said: "Oh, no, I won't call it that. They have had a very hard time." His friend Robin Maugham reported that Churchill even felt "a faint admiration for the electorate's show of independence."

The worst thing at first was the terrible blank. Then the awful frustration. "What I shall miss is this," he said, pointing to the red boxes, still full of state papers. "It is a strange feeling, all power gone. I had made my plans; I feel I could have dealt with things better than anyone else." But a holiday in Italy enabled him to say, "With my painting I have recovered my balance. I'm damned glad now to be out of it." That was September. Yet when he returned home, the effects of "the blow," as he called the election, began to throb again. He was muttering disconsolately, "I'm pretty well played out. I imagine when one folds up like that, this kind of business hits one harder." Did he mean by "this kind of business" what some people have called "the inborn melancholy of the Churchill blood"? Lord Moran had been told of Winston's mood in 1915 following his downfall over Gallipoli. "I'm finished. I'm finished," he kept repeating. It disturbed Moran to think that such a cloud of despondency had hung over him in 1915 when, after all, he was still a young man. That suggested that the roots of Churchill's present depression went deeper than the election defeat, deeper even than old age. How deep?

Facing page: Auld Lang Syne at Potsdam. Churchill, Truman, and Stalin.

Churchill, it must again be emphasised, was a romantic. He liked to gild the highlights and blacken the shadows. When he felt depressed he must describe it as a pitch-black depression. He him-

192

CAMERA PRESS LTD.

POPPERFOTO

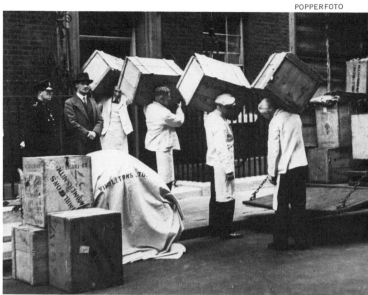

Goodbye to No. 10 Downing Street: leaving the Prime Minister's residence after Churchill's defeat in the 1945 election.

self used the name "Black Dog" for his fits of melancholy. He probably got it from a nurse or maid, perhaps even Mrs. Everest. In the old days, all sorts of folk expressions embedded themselves in the thought and language of children brought up by nannies. The present author had a variant of "Black Dog"—"The Hump." Or rather, "The 'Ump," since the nanny in this case was a cockney who dropped her aitches. "You've got 'The 'Ump,'" she would say ominously. One knew better than to contradict her. Indeed one did not wish to. "The 'Ump" was endured while it lasted with a mixture of gloom and pride.

Whatever the verbal origin of Churchill's "Black Dog," it seems to this writer that he rarely if ever succumbed to it without an adequate reason. Gallipoli, for instance, had a devastating effect upon him. Nearly 30 years later, in regard to the Anzio landings, he was saying, "Anzio was my worst moment in the war. . . . I didn't want two Suvla Bays [Gallipoli]." But did he say it irrationally? The Gallipoli fiasco had indeed come close to ruining his career forever.

If there was also post-election depression in 1945, nothing could have been more natural. His finest hour had ended in total rejection by his countrymen. The Labour landslide against him could be compared only with the Liberal landslide of 1906—except that in 1906, the young Winston had been on the winning side.

This is not to say that Churchill's ebullient temperament did not have its counterpoise of occasional melancholy. But being Churchill, he liked to lay on the "blue" shadows as thickly as Lady Lavery had taught him to lay on the blue paint when he first took up painting after Gallipoli.

The "Black Dog" did afflict Churchill in old age. But for this, the gradual decline of his powers is sufficient explanation. As for the various theories about the melancholy "Churchill blood," some words spoken by Winston Churchill himself put this interesting

194

CENTRAL PRESS PHOTOS LTD.

The triumphant Mr. Attlee. The 1945 election was a landslide victory for Attlee's Labour party. Britain had won the war; now the British people showed themselves determined to win the peace.

question into perspective. "I'm in pretty good fettle," he said to Lord Moran a year after the election. "The Jerome blood," he added.

Perhaps one personal recollection may be injected here. Churchill's hospitable and devoted daughter and son-in-law, Mary and Christopher Soames, were entertaining him and Lady Churchill one Christmas season towards the end of his life. My family and I were invited to dinner. I sat by him, having been kindly warned not to worry if he said nothing. I soon noticed that he ate heartily of the sumptuous Christmas fare; so, thinking to make the conversation equally easy for the old gentleman, I began asking him about some of the British officers in the Boer War and reminded him that one of them had first met him playing soldiers on the nursery floor. But Churchill swept these all aside. He was not interested in the past, he said. Instead he held forth about a new book on Canada and the situation in the Commonwealth.

Churchill's friends agreed with his own diagnosis: that he had quite recovered by 1946 and once more had "a purpose in life." Churchill would not have agreed, however, with those who thought that his "purpose" was only farming, painting, and dictating his *Second World War* at Chartwell. These things he loved, together with his growing family of grandchildren, his poodles Rufus I and II, his budgerigar, golden carp, and foals. But he now had a renewed political purpose and message.

Though he had loudly lamented as early as 1944 that he no longer had a message for the world—except, of course, "fight the damned socialists"—the themes of his post-war message had occurred to him before the war was over. Entitling it "The Sinews of Peace," he delivered it at Fulton, Missouri, to Westminster College on March 5, 1946.

In March, 1946, Churchill made a dramatic return to the international arena, delivering his speech "The Sinews of Peace" at Fulton, Missouri.

POPPERFOTO

The Fulton speech was a call in the grand Churchillian manner for that unity between America and Britain which alone could save the future. Speaking to "this kindred nation" on the whole subject of "these baffling times," he first established his personal links by quoting his old Irish-American friend, Bourke Cockran. If War, Tyranny and Want were the three threats to our civilisation, Cockran believed that Want, at least, could be routed by science. "There is enough for all," Cockran had said. "The earth is a generous mother"—if only people would cultivate her soil "in justice and in peace." So far Churchill felt that he and his American audience were in full agreement.

But what of the other two threats, War and Tyranny? "I come to the crux," said Churchill, "of what I have travelled here to say." Only one thing could ensure the build-up of peace-keeping world organisations, namely, "the fraternal association of the English-speaking peoples. This means a special relationship between the British Commonwealth and Empire and the United States."

196

Next Churchill approached the new menace which the two nations in "special relationship" would have to face—the "iron curtain." This was the part of his Fulton speech which stirred the world. Some were shocked, others galvanised. Though "iron curtain" was an expression used by a German writer and translated in the English *Times* on May 3, 1945, it was Churchill who made it part of the language.

At Fulton he defined the "iron curtain" in characteristic language. "A shadow has fallen upon the scenes so lately lighted by the Allied victory. Nobody knows what Soviet Russia and its Communist international organisation intends to do in the immediate future, or what are the limits if any, to their expansive and proselytising tendencies. . . . From Stettin in the Baltic to Trieste in the Adriatic, an iron curtain has descended across the Continent. Behind that line lie all the capitals of the ancient states of Central and Eastern Europe. Warsaw, Berlin, Prague, Vienna, Budapest, Belgrade, Bucharest and Sofia"—all these famous cities were now lying in the sphere of Soviet influence or even subject to Moscow. Churchill's historical imagination caught fire as the great names rolled off his tongue. In sorrow and anger he declared: "This is certainly not the Liberated Europe we fought to build up. Nor is it one which contains the essentials of permanent peace."

But Churchill had not given up all hope of the Russians. To him, they were a dangerous enigma rather than an irredeemable disaster like Hitler. Of Russia he had once said: "One strokes the nose of the alligator and the ensuing gurgle may be a purr of affection, a grunt of stimulated appetite, or a snarl of enraged animosity. One cannot tell."

The essentials of security against these iron jaws were available to the world nonetheless. Churchill said at Fulton: "The safety of the world requires a new unity in Europe, from which no nation should be permanently outcast." If the alligator turned out to be purring, its presence already inside the United Nations would be doubly welcome. But there was an outcast nation, Germany.

After Fulton came Zurich, and there Churchill enunciated the corollary of his special Anglo-American relationship: Germany restored. At Zurich he called upon France to take Germany by the hand. This was a seminal idea for the future. Churchill also used the phrase at Zurich, "the United States of Europe," though when he regained power in 1951 this concept already meant less to him. His whole championship of European unity sprang not from vague visions of international brotherhood but from the necessity

POPPERFOTO

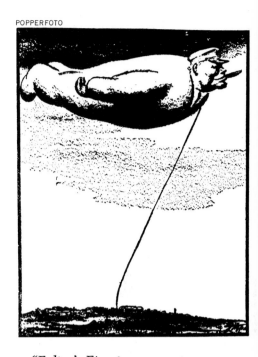

"Fulton's Finest Hour." An American cartoonist's impression of Churchill's speech.

Out with the hounds at Chartwell. As a young man, Churchill had written: "No hour of life is lost that is spent in the saddle."

POPPERFOTO

for reintegrating Germany in the community of nations. Not only was he against the principle of revenge—he denounced the Nuremberg trials in his *Second World War*—but he also felt compassion for Germany's weakness as soon as victory was won. Even when crossing the Rhine with Montgomery and his troops in 1945, he had shuddered to see the look of strain on the faces of German children. Now he was convinced that a strong Germany could be a counterweight to further expansion of influence by Russia.

These speeches at Fulton and Zurich were among his last creative utterances delivered on the old majestic scale.

Yet he still had plentiful honours to reap and a high political duty to perform.

In 1946, he had been awarded the Order of Merit and seven years later he became a Knight of the Garter. (He could have had the Garter much earlier, but declined it while it was still a political honour. When his Queen offered it to him after the Order had been reconstituted as her personal gift, he was enchanted to accept.) Also in 1953, he received the Nobel Prize for Literature.

His four-volume *Marlborough* and his *World Crisis* and *Aftermath* had appeared before the war. He had begun publishing his six-volume history *The Second World War* in 1948. In 1956–58 he was to bring out his four-volume *History of the English-Speaking Peoples*. It is true that few modern historians will allow that he had the power of getting inside the actual past. Indeed, Harold Nicolson, who reviewed Churchill's last book (Volume IV, *The English-Speaking Peoples*), in private considered it "really lamentable." But this is far from saying that Churchill failed as a historian. In his moving oration on the death of Neville Chamberlain, he asked of history that it should at least "kindle with pale gleams the passion of former days." This Churchill achieved most memorably himself. Passion echoes through his pages even though his analyses of its causes and effects may not always satisfy his critics.

Churchill's "Colonist II" wins a race. Once when Colonist II failed to win, Churchill said: "I told him this is a very big race and if you win it, you will never have to run again. You will spend the rest of your life in agreeable female company . . . . Colonist II did not keep his mind on the race."

FOX PHOTOS

Moreover, Churchill used the past sublimely for his own high purposes. It was his passionate feeling for English and American history which made him such a doughty fighter for the great democracies' survival. His American friend Bernard Baruch carried the connection still further. England had three great assets, he said: her Queen, her glorious past—and Winston Churchill. In Churchill's eyes, the first two were inextricably mingled, the Monarchy being the embodiment of England's glorious past. If he himself were a third asset, it would seem so to him only to the extent that he served the other two. As the British Labour leader Aneurin Bevan wrote of him after his death: "History itself seemed to come into that chamber [the House of Commons] and address us. Nobody could have listened and not been moved. This was his *forte*. There has never been anybody who could speak for history as Churchill could."

In the year that he completed his writing, 1958, he became Chairman of the trustees of a new foundation at Cambridge University—Churchill College. It is the first of two national memorials to Sir Winston. The second is the Winston Churchill Memorial Trust to provide for 100 travel scholarships a year.

He himself had suggested the foundation of a college for engineers and scientists and he was touched—and amused—when it was named after him. He said, with a typical pun, "Of course it does seem to put me alongside the Trinity." Churchill College was soon to follow in the steps of its Nobel Prize-winning namesake, for among those who have been associated with the College is a notable list of several American Nobel Prize winners. Its connection with Churchill's family and friends is close. Lady Spencer-Churchill, his widow and since his death a life peeress, was present at the opening of the College's new Archives Centre in 1973 by the American Ambassador to Britain, Walter H. Annenberg. (Churchill made one of his favourite puns about the life peerage: he called it the "disappearage.") His daughters Mary and Sarah were also present, as were his grandson Winston Churchill, M.P., an Honorary Fellow, and his wife. The Bevin Library was given by the Transport and General Workers Union and Trades Union Congress, who wanted the memorial to Ernest Bevin to be contained within the memorial to Churchill. The reading room is a magnificent memorial to his friend Brendan Bracken, who died before him. On one wall hangs a brilliant piece of tapestry given by De Gaulle personally as leader of that country which Churchill always regarded as the cradle of modern civilisation, France.

CONWAY PICTURE LIBRARY

*Winston and Clemmie
with their grandchildren
at Chartwell, 1951.
Left to right: Emma
Soames, Nicholas Soames,
Arabella Churchill.*

To say that the bond between Churchill College and the United States, with its own Winston Churchill Foundation, is strong and always growing stronger, would be a dry version of the reality which is exemplified by the College's latest acquisition. The splendid bronze doors of the Archives Centre, itself built through the generosity of a number of leading Americans, were the gift of seven American companies producing non-ferrous metals, presented "As symbols of their enduring admiration for Sir Winston Churchill." Many of those entering through the doors will bring the best of the United States, the Commonwealth, and much of the rest of the world, into an English college; those leaving will carry the best of England to the United States and many other countries.

———

Meanwhile, in the decade after the war, the world of politics still had much to offer Churchill and he to offer in return.

As Leader of the Opposition, from 1945–51, he did not fail in his duty to oppose Labour. Insofar as Labour was introducing the elements of socialism, such as nationalisation of the railways and power and the creation of a National Health Service, he was against the Government. He asked Lord Moran anxiously: "If Aneurin Bevan becomes Minister of Health, will there be private practice? Will you be able to look after me?" The answer to each question was yes. The prolongation of rationing, even in the interest of fairness, also raised Churchill's ire. He had no sympathy with that austerity for its own sake which he attributed to social-

JOHN SPENCER-CHURCHILL

PAUL MAZE, FROM THE COLLECTION OF LORD CAMROSE

Above, left: A painting of Churchill done by his nephew John Spencer-Churchill after his last broadcast as Prime Minister in 1945. Above, right: Fishing with a young friend. Right: A painter's portrait of Churchill the painter. Asked why he preferred to paint landscapes, Churchill replied: "Because a tree doesn't complain that I haven't done it justice."

PAUL MAZE, FROM THE COLLECTION OF LORD CAMROSE

RADIO TIMES HULTON PICTURE LIBRARY

PAUL MAZE, FROM THE COLLECTION OF LORD CAMROSE

*Above: After his election
defeat in 1945, Churchill had
more time for his writing.
He preferred to dictate at a
standing-desk. Left: Winston
and Clemmie in a relaxed
moment.*

ists. Nor did social reform now set his imagination aflame. During the war, he had focused on one thing and one only, as was his habit—victory. A great social reform like the Beveridge Report of 1942 was to him a distraction. He left it to those in his Cabinet who were interested.

The Report was Sir William Beveridge's famous scheme to provide "social security from the cradle to the grave." Even the friend who perhaps had the most influence upon Churchill, Brendan Bracken, could not get him involved, and all attempts to make him meet Beveridge failed. When the two accidentally met on board the *Queen Mary* sailing to Washington in 1943, Churchill invited Beveridge to lunch at his table—but there the civilities ended. Churchill sat hunched up and scowling at his plate, his thoughts a long way off, says Moran, who was also present. "Besides, his guest on this occasion," adds Moran, "was not particularly congenial. Sir William, no doubt, was conscious that he, too, had done a good job of work for the country. The trouble

Bernard Baruch visits Churchill at Chartwell, 1949.

POPPERFOTO/CONWAY PICTURE LIBRARY

POPPERFOTO

THE PILOT GOES ABOARD AGAIN

POPPERFOTO/CONWAY PICTURE LIBRARY

HOT SEAT

was that this did not occur to the P.M.; at any rate, if it did he kept it to himself, and at about half-past two the bleak little function just petered out."

It was this kind of behaviour (also noted in Wellington and in many other men of genius) which caused Clement Attlee, the Labour Prime Minister from 1945–51, to say of Churchill: "So far as government was concerned, Winston was not a natural democrat. He was an autocrat." Nevertheless, Attlee was not overly distressed by this Churchillian frailty, even though he personally had served as Deputy Prime Minister to Churchill throughout the war and had seen plenty of the great man's temperament. Attlee quoted with leniency amounting to relish a typically Churchillian remark made to him one day in the Cabinet room: "Of course I am an egotist," said Churchill. "Where do you get if you aren't?"

Churchill was to get back as Prime Minister in October, 1951, with Anthony Eden (the future Lord Avon) as his Deputy. Parts of the superlative human machine were showing signs of wear and tear. He could not always remember faces or names. One anecdote related by Nicolson illustrates this situation in an amusing way. Reflecting on Britain's part in the Korean War in 1950, while he was still Leader of the Opposition, Churchill had said to a group of friends: "The old man is very good to me. I could not have managed this situation had I been in Attlee's place. I should have

Prime Minister once more. Left, "John Bull" watches with satisfaction as Churchill climbs aboard. Right, the three defeated Labour Ministers are Attlee, Herbert Morrison, and Hugh Gaitskell. With Churchill are Conservatives Eden and R. A. Butler.

205

been called a warmonger." "What old man?" asked an M.P., David Maxwell Fyfe. "God, Sir Donald," replied Churchill. He always called David Maxwell Fyfe "Sir Donald."

Besides illustrating his weakness over names, the story also shows his attitude towards religion. He never discussed religious questions except in a lighthearted tone. When asked on his 75th birthday, for instance, whether he was afraid of death, he answered: "I am ready to meet my Maker. Whether my Maker is prepared for the great ordeal of meeting me is another matter." His tone might always be bantering, but it is clear from the Nicolson story that he believed in providence, and a providence with which he hoped to have, as with the United States, a "special relationship."

Forming his new Government was a strain. "I have had to fill seventy-five offices—it has worried me, particularly the junior appointments. If anyone is left out, it is probably the end of his political hopes. You know [to Moran] how unhappy it makes me to hurt others." He heaved a deep sigh. "The last fortnight has been more tiring than anything in the war. There were great decisions then, of course, but I was swept along by events."

Alas, Churchill's all-time inspiration, events, now often seemed confusing and elusive. Instead of being swept along by them, he had to steer cautiously to avoid capsising. The interest which Churchill had proclaimed at Fulton in an international defence force waned. He even described the European Defence Community as "a sludgy amalgam." Once West Germany had become a friend, he felt that the European idea had fulfilled its main purpose.

At the same time, a new event was haunting his imagination— an evil and poisonous event—the Cold War. Churchill was to spend the rest of his political life in seeking the antidote. He made it his last great service to humanity to work for peace with Soviet Russia. Stalin's death on March 5, 1953, made his task easier. Characteristically, he refused to join in mud-slinging at his old wartime comrade. If Churchill had been younger and Roosevelt had lived to assess the needs of the fifties, they might together have brought the Cold War to an end.

But there was now a cold war going on within Churchill's own physical frame. On one side, nature in rebellion; on the other, an indomitable will to survive. Occasionally, his personal cold war would flare up into a crisis, and his great spirit would be on the point of extinction.

THE PRESS ASSOCIATION LTD.

*Churchill sets off for
America on December 29,
1951, with his doctor,
Lord Moran. Below:
Churchill addresses
Congress; seated behind
him are Vice-President
Alben Barkley and
Speaker of the House
Sam Rayburn.*

POPPERFOTO

POPPERFOTO

King George VI died in February, 1952. The Government's floral wreath carried the words "For Gallantry," the simple inscription on the George Cross, a new Order instituted by the King himself.

In August, 1949, he had had his first stroke. He was still only Leader of the Opposition and on holiday with Max Beaverbrook at Monte Carlo. Within a short while, though he was 74, the enemy had been routed.

The next time was in February, 1952. But now Churchill was Prime Minister, and though the illness—disturbance of cerebral circulation—was slight, the problems involved were obviously more serious. A week or two before the attack, Churchill had been at his best. He had made a moving broadcast on the death of King George VI. The ailing King had "walked with Death and made Death his friend," said Churchill. Then, on February 21, Churchill picked up the telephone and suddenly could not think of the right words. "Am I going to have a stroke?" he asked Moran. Must he too learn to walk with death?

Not yet. A year later he was in full force again, perhaps to match the morning glory of his young idol, the new Queen. "Lovely, inspiring," was how he described Queen Elizabeth II. Her Coronation brought him an excuse for much agreeable interference with unimaginative official arrangements. He was all for jollity. The officials were proposing to give the people in the stands by Byron's statue, for example, plenty of toilets but no refreshments. "Looking after their exports while neglecting their imports," said Churchill with a wicked grin.

On June 24, 1953, he had another, severe stroke while at an official dinner, and just after having delivered most effective words of welcome to Italy's Prime Minister. Both his speech and his gait were affected. Moreover, his Deputy, Anthony Eden, had flown to Boston for a serious operation. Churchill planned to attend a world conference at Bermuda; this now had to be postponed. But within a month he was already staging a comeback. On August 18, he presided over his first Cabinet meeting since the stroke, and nobody noticed anything wrong. Nevertheless, it hardly seemed possible that by December he should be attending the Bermuda Conference. There he proposed friendly gestures towards Russia, including personal contacts and trade agreements. And six months later, June, 1954, he was paying visits to Washington and Ottawa. Such were the results of his inflexible resolve.

In Washington, he had been up to the hilt in speaking, broadcasting, arguing. "I do not feel at all tired," he said, glorying in the strenuousness of his program. "There is something in the magnetism of this great portion of the earth's surface which always makes me feel buoyant." Moran called his performance in Wash-

POPPERFOTO

CHORUS: *Unfurl the flags and sound the trumpets loud,*
    For today we march again,
As the soldiers of a noble and proud
    Elizabethan reign,
       Elizabethan reign.

VERSE 1: *We hear the echoes of distant years ago*
    When hostile peoples arrayed our countryside,
Raleigh defended our island from the foe,
    And Drake sailed his vessels against the Spanish pride.

Unfurl the flags, etc. . . .

VERSE 2: *Ours is the duty to stand as sentinel,*
    We are entrusted with defending the free,
Aiding the vanquished and from our citadel
    We shall fight our battles for lasting victory.

Unfurl the flags, etc. . . .

VERSE 3: *We are the heralds of a new born yesterday,*
    We are the guardians of a past and glorious scene,
We are an army again in fine array
    And bearing the standards of our most gracious Queen.

Unfurl the flags, etc. . . .

Above, the Prime Minister visits Harrow. Left, the verses to a coronation march written by his nephew John Spencer-Churchill for Churchill's installation as a Knight of the Garter. The music and verses are in the style of Harrow songs, of which Churchill was so fond.

John S. Churchill
April, 1953

POPPERFOTO

Anthony Eden and his bride, Clarissa Spencer-Churchill, niece of the Prime Minister, leaving No. 10 Downing Street for their honeymoon. Left to right: the bride, John Spencer-Churchill, the Prime Minister, the Prime Minister's daughter Diana Sandys, Clementine Churchill, Mr. Eden. August, 1952.

ington a "wonderful *tour de force*." He went on to Ottawa, delivering another of his impressive messages: "Canada is the master link of Anglo-Saxon unity." The people cheered him wildly all along the route. "I liked it very much," he said on the way home; "I purred like a cat."

This was the highest possible compliment. He loved cats. He used to invite his favourite, the Marmalade Cat, to sit up to table so that he might carry on a Churchillian "conversation" with it on the political problems of the day.

Then, on November 30, 1954, came his 80th birthday. Both Houses of Parliament and all parties combined to present him with a portrait of himself by the outstanding painter Graham Sutherland. The ceremony took place in Westminster Hall, whose glorious hammerbeam roof dates back to the reign of Richard II. No one who was present will ever forget the dramatic contrasts of the scene—tension, mischief, affection, deep solemnity—many of them supplied by the hero himself. Sutherland's striking portrait presented Churchill as the furious lion at bay. It was not the version of himself which he had expected to go down in history. When the picture was unveiled, there was a moment of suspense. The scowl on his face matched the lion's in the picture—until a familiar twinkle appeared and the growls dissolved in a crow of merriment. "The portrait is a remarkable example of modern art," he began. "It certainly combines force and candour." He had released us all in laughter.

He wound up with the most personal manifesto of his life, already quoted in this book. "It was the nation and the race dwelling all round the globe that had the lion's heart. I had the luck to be called upon to give the roar."

His old wartime colleague Attlee, now Leader of the Opposition, was moved on this occasion to exorcise the blackest demon of Winston's past. "You had the conception of the Dardanelles campaign," said Attlee, "the only imaginative strategic idea of the [first world] war. I wish that you had had full power to carry it to success."

So Gallipoli had been publicly justified at last. Churchill nodded his head. He left the great hall with tears in his eyes.

With the spear pulled out of the Gallipoli wound, the ancient warrior should no doubt have died quickly and quietly. But

Churchill's 82nd birthday. With Arabella Churchill, daughter of Randolph.

POPPERFOTO

Winston was more than unpredictable. He was obdurate. He had once said, "We will never surrender;" and now those who thought the old lion would surrender his office found unmistakable signs that he intended to carry on. However, there was another of his wartime sayings, "Give us the tools and we will finish the job." Alas, the tools of his trade, the magnificent energy, industry, and memory, were slipping out of his hands. The job of reaching agreement with Russia must be finished by other hands, even by another generation.

When the general election of spring, 1955, approached, he realised that his time had come. The Queen and Prince Philip gave him an evening of intense romantic happiness by dining with him and Lady Churchill at No. 10 Downing Street. Then, on April 5, he resigned.

To everyone's amazement there was life in the old lion yet.

Churchill is installed as a Knight of the Garter in 1954. He once said he would have liked the honour but without the "Sir." Why not a "discourtesy" title of "Mister," since his father had had the courtesy title of "Lord"?

POPPERFOTO

FOX PH

Churchill's retirement in 1955 was announced on a newssheet because of a newspaper strike at the time.

Ten more years, to be precise, in which to gather up a tremendous harvest of love and veneration. They were years of apotheosis rather than of sunset, wrote his friend Jock Colville. Shining among the gods, he no longer needed to reach for a star. He had become one.

In his 88th year, he was made an honorary citizen of the United States, surely another "finest hour." One ray of his genius dazzled the "kindred nation" beyond all others. He personified the right to be free. On April 9, 1963, in language as noble as Churchill's own, President John F. Kennedy spoke at the White House ceremony: "We meet to honor a man whose honor requires no meeting—for he is the most honored and honorable man to walk the stage of human history in the time in which we live." Then the President went on to name Churchill's two greatest services to mankind: his "zest for freedom" and the war-winning musketry of

Sir Winston opens the car door for Queen Elizabeth II as she and Prince Philip leave No. 10 Downing Street after dining with the Churchills on the eve of the Prime Minister's retirement.

POPPERFOTO

POPPERFOTO/CONWAY PICTURE LIBRARY

Above: Churchill's 90th birthday cake, with his motto inscribed. Below: Churchill was made an honorary citizen of the United States in 1963.

his speeches. "Whenever and wherever tyranny threatened he has always championed liberty . . . he has served all men's freedom and dignity . . . . he mobilized the English language and sent it into battle."

Twenty years earlier, Churchill had broached the idea at Harvard University of a common Anglo-American citizenship for the two democracies, but he was content to leave this to time. Meanwhile, he had told Adlai Stevenson in jest that he, Churchill, was "an English-speaking Union" in himself. Now he could say it in truth. They all felt, as indeed they said, he was "truly *one of us*;" not just because he was half American, but because "he helped us to fight for our freedom." Never had so many owed so much to one man.

Miraculously, he was not to have another stroke until the final one, which occurred a fortnight before he died on January 24, 1965. This fortnight in itself seemed to Moran little short of a miracle. How could a stricken man of over 90 cling on? Each night must surely be Winston's last. "But Winston had never taken orders from anyone. He had always been unpredictable; he was to be like that to the end."

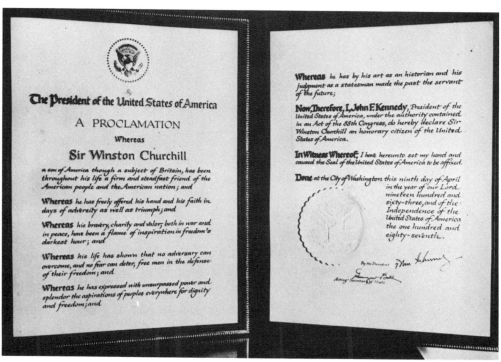

POPPERFOTO

KARSH, OTTAWA/CAMERA PRESS LTD.

He lay in a coma for those 14 days. Yet, as Lytton Strachey wrote of the dying Queen Victoria, perhaps in the secret chambers of consciousness, he had his thoughts, too. Perhaps his fading mind "called up once more the shadows of the past to float before it, and retrace, for the last time, the vanished visions of that long history—passing back and back, through the cloud of years, to older and ever older memories"—to Stalin at Potsdam, drinking toast after toast in tiny glasses, and the Buckingham Palace balcony on V-E Day, and Monty in his caravan, and Sarah and Mary in their uniforms, and Roosevelt at the White House in the intense heat of summer, giving him a room delightfully irrigated with streams of cool air, and the vapour trail of a Spitfire, and the thrum of invisible German bombers, and the golden carp at Chartwell, and Gandhi's queer diet, and Kitchener's queer eyes, and Jacky Fisher's scarlet labels saying "RUSH," and Lloyd George charming the birds out of the trees, and the besieged house in Sidney Street, and Clemmie signing a letter with a "Kat," and the Boers' slouch hats, and the whites of the Dervishes' eyes, and the school songs at Harrow, and patting Papa's hunter in Ireland, and climb-

Churchill (and his cat Jock) at the wedding of his grandson Winston Churchill. Front row (l-r): the bride, Minnie d'Erlanger; Sir Winston; the groom; Arabella Churchill. Back row: Lady Churchill; Hon. Mrs. Hayward; Sir Winston's daughter Mary Soames; Mr. Douglas Wilson.

215

Mail for "The Greatest Man Alive." Two unusually addressed greetings which were received by Sir Winston on his 90th birthday.

FOX PHOTOS

ing on to Woomany's comfortable lap, and a diamond like the evening star in his mother's hair, and the lake and lawns at Blenheim.

Pomp and Circumstance, Elgar's march, had been played in Westminster Hall for Winston Churchill in 1954. Now in 1965, the catafalque lay in Westminster Hall for three days; on the fourth it was carried with due pomp and circumstance to St. Paul's Cathedral. He had asked for a soldier's funeral. So on January 30, the coffin was placed on a gun carriage drawn by 100 sailors of the Royal Navy, with a detachment of the Royal Air Force as escort. Bearer parties were formed by Her Majesty's Brigade of Guards. A Union Jack covered the coffin on which were laid the insignia of the Order of the Garter. Guards of Honour were formed at strategic points by the Navy, Army, and Air Force. "Big Ben" struck 9:45 a.m.; the procession started; and for the rest of the day, the clock which dominated the Houses of Parliament was silent. But the boom of minute guns could be heard from St. James's Park and the Tower of London.

Eight bands led the procession through the packed streets, with men from the Services marching between them. Two more bands followed the coffin. Awaiting the coffin in the Cathedral were the Royal Family and a vast congregation, including representatives of the United States and the Soviet Union. At least by his funeral Churchill had brought about a truce in the Cold War.

Nothing so splendid, so imposing, so overwhelming had been seen since Wellington's funeral a century ago; indeed, the six giant candelabra which had once stood around Wellington's coffin were now to stand around Churchill's. Purple Staff Officers con-

216

ducted the people to their seats. Pursuivants, Heralds, Kings of Arms, all in their medieval costumes, marched in procession up the Cathedral. Churchill's orders and decorations, the banner of the Cinque Ports, of which he had been Warden, and the banner of Spencer-Churchill were borne by officers of the Hussars. The ten pallbearers had all served with Churchill during the war, either in the armed forces or in the Government—from Avon to Alexander, from Attlee to Mountbatten.

As the solemn "Sentences" died away under the dome, Bunyan's hymn rang out loud and strong:

> *Who would true valour see,*
> *Let him come hither;*
> *One here will constant be,*
> *Come wind, come weather....*

We felt that the ancient words had somehow been written for Churchill and no other. And we suddenly saw that Churchill's "first avowed intent," even if it had sometimes seemed a very human intent to be great, to shine, to be first, was all along, in the words of the hymn, "to be a pilgrim."

He would have wept with emotion, as was his way, to hear the theme of valour maintained throughout the two great hymns which followed, *The Battle Hymn of the Republic* and *Fight the Good Fight*. Churchill, we felt, had known more about "the grapes of wrath" than most of us, and about "the fateful lightning" and "the terrible swift sword." He, if anyone, had had the right to say, "let us die to make men free."

As for the last hymn, *O God Our Help in Ages Past*, here, perhaps, some of the words were not as appropriate.

> *Time like an ever-rolling stream*
> *Bears all its sons away.*
> *They fly forgotten, as a dream*
> *Dies at the opening day.*

Like dreams most of us would indeed "fly forgotten." He would be remembered. The Last Post sounded. There was a brief silence. Then, *Reveille*.

It was possible also to wonder if the human being—that amusing, loveable, mischievous, delectable being—would be lost in all this sublime ceremony. On and on it went. Handel's *Dead March*, the Mourning Sword carried by the Lord Mayor in front of the Queen, the aerial salute as the launch *Havengore,* now carrying the coffin, and attendant launches travelled up the River Thames towards Waterloo Station.

But the human touches were not missing. General Eisenhower's message, broadcast at the very moment that Churchill's mortal remains were moving upon "the mighty Thames," avenue of history, struck a note both profound and human. "In the coming years, many in countless words will strive to interpret the motives, describe the accomplishments, and extol the virtues of Winston Churchill—soldier, statesman, and citizen that two great countries were proud to claim as their own. Among all the things so written or spoken, there will ring out through all the centuries one incontestable refrain: He was a champion of freedom. . . . And now to you, Sir Winston—my old friend—farewell."

There had also been the delightful figure of a small grandchild in a scarlet coat, among all the rows of black. There was frail Lord Attlee after it was over, sitting on a kitchen chair (someone had kindly brought it) in the biting wind on the edge of the pavement, looking sad and thoughtful as he waited for his car. Churchill would have liked that little scene. Above all there was the burial in Bladon churchyard, near Blenheim.

The date of Winston Churchill's death was to be precisely the same as his father's—January 24. Churchill had forecast this date to Jock Colville in 1954, making the coincidence seem almost predestined. Had not the son decided several years earlier to be buried beside his father, mother, and brother, Jack, the hero's remains assuredly would have been lowered into the same vault with Nelson and Wellington, lapped in pomp and circumstance and the roll of the Cathedral organ right to the very end. Churchill chose instead a private interment in a country churchyard.

On the final journey by train to Long Handborough, the station for Bladon, the mood seemed already to have changed from glory to simple affection. A man was seen standing at attention on the flat roof of his house wearing his old R.A.F. uniform and saluting; in a field beside the track, a farmer stood bareheaded as the funeral train passed.

When all was said and done, what were the tributes for?

For being the saviour of Western civilisation; for his championship of freedom; for being the greatest leader in war Britain has ever known; for the breadth of his world statesmanship, with his special devotion to the United States; for truly belonging, like

Lincoln, to the ages; for the galvanic effect of his language; for saying "Trust the People," like his father before him; for being "us as we would like the world to see us;" for harnessing the past to the present as a great artist in politics; for his wit, humour, and imagination; for his irresistible charm; for his engaging foibles; for his love of bright colours in life, as in painting; for the goodness, kindness, and compassion which were never far beneath the surface, however ruffled that surface might be; for his magnanimity; for his vitality, energy, and longevity, all expressions of his life force; for his concentration on the essentials; for his perseverance; for his moral courage; for his indomitable spirit. "For Valour."

Randolph Churchill stands beside a statue of his father after the unveiling ceremony at the British Embassy in Washington, April, 1966. The statue stands with one foot on British Embassy land, the other in the U.S.A.

POPPERFOTO

Afterword

THIS BOOK was written at the suggestion of the Winston Churchill Foundation of the United States, an organisation established in 1959 as an expression of American admiration for my grandfather. It seems appropriate to say something about this Foundation, of which I have the honour of being a Trustee, and whose important programmes carried on in honour of Winston Churchill are too little known.

In the last years of his life, my grandfather, regarded by the world for his contribution to politics and history, war and statecraft, oratory and painting, was especially interested in fostering scientific and technological education. He knew, at first hand, the role of science and technology in war; they had provided the implements by which freedom had been preserved. He believed deeply that they could also help assure the forward march of mankind towards those "broad, sunlit uplands" of peace and prosperity of which he so frequently spoke. Although he was born and grew to manhood before the emergence of modern technology, he was keenly sensitive to the challenge of the new age. He was especially admiring of how Americans had harnessed scientific and technological talent to their economy. He had been greatly impressed by a visit he made in 1948 to the Massachusetts Institute of Technology in Boston and he was determined to see established in Britain a college of technology of comparable standing. The result was Churchill College, Cambridge, which he founded in 1959. The College, which has become Britain's National Memorial to Winston Churchill, has earned an enviable academic reputation in little more than a decade.

When the Trustees of the Winston Churchill Foundation of the United States sought a way to create an enduring American memorial to my grandfather, they concluded they could do nothing more significant, nor more pleasing to him, than to sponsor a programme which would at once foster scientific and technical education in the United States, encourage cooperation in these areas between the United States and Britain, and thus strengthen the bonds of unity between the two countries which Winston Churchill symbolised.

Accordingly, with funds contributed from American corporations, foundations, and individuals, the Churchill Foundation initiated two programmes: a scholarship programme, under which the most promising young graduates of leading American colleges and universities are enabled to do graduate study in engineering, mathematics, and science at Churchill College; and a fellowship programme, which permits distinguished American scholars, primarily, but not exclusively, in the sciences, to spend a period of time at Churchill College in research, study, or writing. The fact that seven Churchill Fellows have won Nobel Prizes may be taken as an indication of the Foundation's standards.

To date, the Churchill Foundation has sponsored almost 200 Scholars and Fellows. By their own testimony, they have profited immensely from their experiences in England. Their advanced studies have been academically and professionally rewarding. And perhaps no less important, "their horizons of international understanding," to use my grandfather's words, have been enlarged. I must hasten to add that the benefits have been mutual. Not only Churchill College, but Cambridge University, and, it is no exaggeration to say, all Britain profit from the presence in their midst of such talented and distinguished American men and women. The interaction between the American Scholars and Fellows and their British colleagues has enriched teaching and research in both countries and has encouraged that mutual understanding and, one may hope, appreciation which sustain the common heritage of these two great English-speaking democracies.

My grandfather was enthusiastic in his support of the Foundation's plans when they were formulated. I know that he would have been equally enthusiastic and gratified at the results of the Foundation's work. With that conviction, the Trustees of the Winston Churchill Foundation of the United States in this his Centenary year have launched an appeal for one million dollars to endow the Foundation on an enduring basis for the future.

I also think it safe to say that my grandfather would have been very pleased at this book and its review of his life, which was long and, as he put it in an address to a joint session of Congress, "not entirely uneventful."

Winston S. Churchill
June 6, 1974

Index

PRINTED IN U.S.A.